IMMORTALITY
&
REINCARNATION

IMMORTALITY
&
REINCARNATION

ALEXANDRA DAVID-NEEL

Translated by Jon Graham

Inner Traditions
Rochester, Vermont

Inner Traditions International
One Park Street
Rochester, Vermont 05767
www.InnerTraditions.com

Library of Congress Cataloging-in-Publication Data
David-Neel, Alexandra, 1868-1969.
 [Immortalité et réincarnation. English]
 Immortality & reincarnation / Alexandra David-Neel ; translated by
Jon Graham.
   p.   cm.
 Includes index.
 ISBN 978-0-89281-619-4 (alk. paper)
  1. Immortality—Comparative studies. 2. Reincarnation—
Comparative studies. I. Title.
BL530.D37   1997
291.2'3—dc2I   97-2446
                                                         CIP

Printed and bound in the United States

10 9

Text design and layout by Kristin Camp
This book was typeset in Centaur with Schneidler as the display typeface

CONTENTS

PREFACE

VOCABULARY IS NOT SHELTERED FROM THE WHIMS OF FASHION. Certain words age. As they cease to be written or heard, they fall into oblivion. Others find themselves suddenly in vogue. Writers and speakers make wide use of them at every turn. The term *problem* is currently among this group. Could this be a response to the particularly gripping concerns that currently prey upon us?

A problem consists of a question that is resolved by finding a solution. It also suggests something that counters our desires and signifies a quest for the proper means of surmounting the obstacle and attaining the desired objective.

Accordingly, it is normal to hear talk of political, economic, and religious problems, among countless others, but there is a problem rarely cited that nonetheless remains at the foreground of our conscious and subconscious concerns. It reveals itself under multiple disguises, both in the collective life of society and in the individual physical and mental life of each one of us. This problem is eternal life.

The idea of ceasing to exist is odious and horribly painful to every individual. No matter how low his station in life, the individual

longs with all his might to endure for a long time, to live on indefinitely and eternally.

The problem of eternal life is intimately linked to the ego. It is
evident that the idea one has of the ego and the manner in which its
mental representation has been fashioned dictate the conceptions
of which modes of duration are applicable to it.

Ask any individual: "You wish to continue after death, perhaps
you believe that you will continue? But what in reality is that thing
you want to continue? What is it, according to you, that continues
to exist after death?" It is probable that your respondent will find
these questions absurd or, at least, that a great number of those you
ask will find them ridiculous. Isn't the response quite simple? "It is
my duration that I want," or "It's *I* that will continue to exist," those
questioned will respond, according to their religious or philosophical convictions.

Your duration? What are you, *you*? What does this *you* consist of?
When you say: "It's *I* that desires to continue to exist," what is this *I*?

For the majority of westerners, whether they follow the definition provided by their catechisms—"man is composed of a mortal
body and an immortal *soul*"—or analogous meanings that establish
a well-defined division between spirit and matter, it is not a subject
that is up for discussion. It's the principle of immateriality: the soul
continues to exist even though the body is destroyed. The same does
not apply to those who subscribe to different notions concerning
the constitution of their person.

However, in all situations, reality imposes on man the deposition
of the transitory character of all that surrounds him. But this painful verification does not prevail over his innate desire for immortality. He is stubbornly persistent, creating myths, doctrines, and practices that are all intended to comfort him and confirm his cherished
faith in his own immortality.

To be complete, the investigations of this subject should be extended to all peoples. This is beyond the measure of my capabilities and certainly extends well beyond the framework of this book. Detailed information can be gleaned from the scholarly works of specialists of the different civilizations. I will confine myself here to territory that is familiar to me: China, India, and Tibet.

CHINA

✦

TAOISM IS AN EXCELLENT EXAMPLE OF A CHINESE PHILOSOPHY that includes a belief in immortality. In our time Taoism is hardly more than a blend of beliefs and practices borrowed from ancient Chinese religion and popular Buddhism. What was the original Taoist philosophy as it existed several centuries before Christ?[1] One would think that it resembled Indian Vedanta at numerous points. However, I am not proposing to trace the history of Taoism here but rather to examine some of the ways in which Taoist adepts and those of the Chinese more or less akin to them have envisioned the problem of survival after death and its solution.

First of all, let's look at how Taoism represents the world in which man has emerged.

Taoism does not envision a *veritable* beginning of the universe, an absolute commencement. Our world is nothing but a mode, a phase of "Existence in Itself," the Tao, which no word can describe nor any thought comprehend.[2] The beginning of our world is located in

---

1. Approximately 300–400 B.C.

2. "The Tao which can be named is not the eternal Tao" (Tao Te Ching).

the chaos from which all emerged originally and to which everything will be integrated anew. Chaos exists periodically. Intervals of
inconceivable duration separate the periods in which the world exists from those in which it dissolves back into chaos. A latent energy exists within this chaos: respiration. Exhalation, or breath, creates all that exists. If one doesn't fear to employ a rather singular
phraseology it could be said that the world, emanating from chaos,
has been "breathed" into the void.[3]

These energy-breaths contained within chaos are mirrored in
movement. They divide and combine while passing from a purely
subtle state to one that gradually becomes more and more material.
The more subtle substances rise and form the sky, while those that
have attained a state of gross matter descend and form the earth. It
is from these inferior breaths that man is made.

These breaths are not inert. They possess their own form of vi-
tality. However, that which truly animates the human body is a pure
breath (with no extraneous elements) emanating directly from the
Tao. Through embodiment, this pure breath blends with the grosser
elements that constitute the material substance of the body. It is the
separation of this superior breath from these grosser elements that
causes death.

None of the constituent elements of the individual assemblage is

---

3. In fact this expression was used by an adept who spoke with me. Compare it to
the teachings found in the Hindu Vedantas: "All things visible emerge from the
invisible at the approach of day. When night returns they melt back into this
same Invisibility" (Bhagavad Gîtâ 8:18). "Thus live and relive the entire assembly
of beings turn by turn. But beyond this visible nature exists another, invisible,
eternal, when all the individuals perish they do not perish, they are called Invisible and Indivisible" (Bhagavad Gîtâ 8:19). "At the end of the Kalpa the beings
return into my creative potency, at the beginning of the Kalpa I emit them anew"
(Bhagavad Gîtâ 10:7).

intrinsically immortal. The man who is infatuated with immortality must create his own. There has never been a Taoist conception of an immortal principle separate from the physical body. Therefore, the objective is to make the body immortal since it is this immortal body that will continue to serve as a habitation for the spirit. Such an undertaking is arduous, but the ancient *Tao-sses*[4] believed themselves capable of pursuing it to good effect as long as they persevered in their efforts.

The existence of both male and female Immortals is beyond any doubt for Chinese Taoists and even for a great number of Chinese in general. Though it is rare to hear tales of encounters with these Immortals in our day, incidents of this kind are often mentioned in the works of ancient authors. These contain descriptions of long pilgrimages by virtuous Taoists seeking the Immortals, impelled by the desire of being taught transcendent truths.

The Immortals didn't inhabit extraterrestrial regions like the gods. Certain places in the mountains and certain islands are thought to be occasional, if not permanent, shelters for them. These pilgrims didn't wander totally at random; those desirous of meeting them would direct themselves toward these locations. And, we are told, they were sometimes successful in their quests.

Among the isles supposedly inhabited by the Immortals, three are commonly mentioned: P'ang Tai, Fang Tchang, and Ying Tcheou, which are said to be located off of the Gulf of Pecheli. It would seem easy enough to reach them, but according to the chronicles, aspiring visitors were assailed by storm and shipwreck when they tried to land on them.

---

4. It is generally acceptable to apply the denomination *Taoist* to all sects of the Taoist doctrine and to reserve the term *Tao-sse* for the adepts initiated into Taoism's profound teachings and the practices arising therefrom.

Various expeditions were sent during the reign of the Tsinn dynasty. None of these reached its goal, and among these only the members of one expedition claimed to have even caught sight of the isles. However, we have other accounts coming from people who claimed to have reached these isles and been welcomed there by the Immortals. Moreover, many of these encounters with the Immortals are said to have occurred in the interior of the country, in the mountains, or even among the crowded cities. Like genies, the Immortals would promenade in the guise of ordinary individuals, and only those endowed with superior faculties of clairvoyance were capable of recognizing them.

Among the countless stories relating the events of the quest for the Elixir of Immortality can be cited that of Magician Lu and Emperor Tche Houang Ti. These events would have occurred circa 222 B.C. Several versions exist of this tale, but we will only recount that part of it pertaining to a belief in the existence of the Immortals. It stands out in the accounts preserved in Chinese chronicles that these Immortals were sometimes believed to be men who had successfully achieved eternal life and sometimes thought to be naturally immortal genies.

The Magician Lu is assumed to have been a disciple of the famous Master Kâo. The latter had been dead for several centuries but was believed by some to have contrived his disappearance and to be still living somewhere in the mountains, having become an Immortal. The emperors even sent emissaries to find him on several occasions.

Among other theories, Kâo professed that it was possible to become immortal by shedding the body much in the same way that insects shed a cocoon. How this result could be obtained wasn't explained. However, even if these instructions never came down to us, it is still very likely that the master supplied them to his immediate disciples. In any event, the ascension to immortality has been especially attributed to the absorption of certain special elixirs. There are exceptional cases cited where virtuous men and sages have received this marvelous elixir as a gift from the Immortals, but in general its manufacture was considered to be the work of alchemist magicians.

The Magician Lu said to the emperor: "My envoys and I have tried in vain to meet the Immortals from whom we could obtain the beverage of immortality for you. But it appears that evil spirits[5] were throwing obstacles in our path. According to the rules of magic the emperor would have to remain invisible so that the enemy spirits couldn't see him, and thus the idea of thwarting his plans wouldn't occur to them."[6]

Following the advice that was given to him, the emperor locked himself away in his palace. After this point Chinese chroniclers have abandoned themselves to all manner of wild speculations. Certain writers maintain that the emperor possessed a hundred palaces surrounded by vast parks and connected to each other by galleries so Tche Houang Ti could go from one to another without being seen. Darker tales speak of one immense palace constructed to resemble the various residences of the gods. Historians of a more rational inclination present Tche Houang Ti as a shrewd politician who fooled the people into thinking he was locked away in his palace in order to devote himself to alchemical research, whereas in truth he wandered the country in disguise. There he observed what was going on and inspected the activities of his officials. However, once in possession of this information, he didn't make the mistake of revealing himself by suppressing those he judged inclined to thwart his plans, even those capable of hatching plots against him.

In addition to the stories concerning quests for the Immortals,

---

5. The *koei* are evil spirits. At times, at the death of an individual, when the different souls separate, certain of the inferior souls become *koei*.

6. Deceiving the evil spirits by ruses to hide one from their sight is a practice common in Tibet.

Chinese chronicles are also replete with examples in which this or that Taoist adept was blessed by the unexpected visit of an Immortal. Personally, I have known a Taoist writer, a serious man whose education had familiarized him with modern science and an individual hardly inclined to indulge himself with fantasies and daydreams. However, he believed that his own spiritual teacher, who resided from time to time in the area of Omishan[7] and met with his disciples there, was one of these Immortals.

Whatever the case may have been in the past concerning the belief in these Immortals and to whatever extent it persists into modern times, the case of the Immortals has always been considered as exceptional. Therefore, we will turn our attention to more current conceptions concerning the fate of the dead.

According to Taoists, the individual contains within his body several souls. These include three superior souls: the *houen* and seven inferior souls: the *p'o*. These souls can be considered individual entities that enjoy a more or less independent existence and are not immaterial, though composed of a substance that is more subtle than that which makes up the body. At the death of an individual, these different souls disperse without ceasing to exist. According to one opinion, this dispersion is the actual cause of death.

Various theories abound on the subject of the fate of the souls who have left the body in which they lived. On one point they are all in agreement: this fate is not a happy one.

Even though in principle each of the three superior souls can pursue their individual destinies, there are few details available about them. For a number of centuries, without making a distinction among the three houen, the Chinese have believed that the souls of the majority of the dead descend into an underground region called the Yellow Springs, where they are detained. This is a dark and lugubrious realm but it isn't hell.

---

7. Omishan is a sacred mountain located in the Chinese province of Szechwan.

The suffering felt by the disembodied soul is regret for the body from which it has been separated. Even though it is not totally deprived of a somewhat material envelope, the lack of a physical body creates a painful situation. It desires to feel the sensations that it knew when it was still joined to a body and feels the need to accomplish certain actions that were habitual to it. It can now satisfy neither of these wishes since it lacks the necessary limbs and organs.

How long does the soul persist in these miserable conditions? The information concerning this subject is not very precise. The same applies to the fate of the inferior souls, the p'o. The latter either lurk around the tomb in which their former body lies or haunt the house in which it lived. Embittered by the disagreeable situation in which they find themselves, they are believed to become easily irritated and are prompt to turn ill-humored—and even openly hostile—toward the living before they disintegrate.

The superior soul of greater consciousness that is confined to the country of the Yellow Springs cannot subsist there indefinitely once separated from a material body. It strives to find another to replace the one it has lost and to resume its place among the living. Friends and parents torture themselves with thoughts of its suffering, but first they strive to dissuade the soul from quitting this world. In little Chinese villages where the old customs persist, I have seen peasants climbing up on their rooftops appealing to the soul of one of their neighbors, whose body was laid out inside, to linger there until the day of the funeral.

A text dating from the third century B.C., translated by the great Sinologist Maspero[8] and entitled *The Recall of the Soul,* poetically expresses the beliefs and feelings entertained by the Chinese on the fate of disembodied souls:

---

8. 1846–1916.

O soul, come back! Having quit the body of your lord, what are you
    doing in the four directions?
O soul, come back! Don't entrust yourself to the East!
Those souls there are pursued by the Man who is a Thousand Cubits
    Long.
The ten suns follow behind him, they melt metal, they liquify the rocks.
They are accustomed to such heat but the soul who lives there will be
    liquified.
Soul, come back! You musn't entrust yourself to that region!
O Soul, come back! You mustn't stop in the South!
The Tattooed Foreheads and the "Black-Teeth" offer sacrifices of human
    flesh there
And with the bones they make a broth.
It is the country of vipers, serpents, and one-hundred league pythons
The male nine-headed hydra comes and goes there, quickly and suddenly
And swallowing men makes his heart sing.
O soul, come back! In the West the danger is the moving sands that are a
    thousand leagues large
If in your spinning you enter the Source of Thunder, you will be pulver-
    ized. Don't stay there!
If by chance you escape, it is surrounded by nothing but a sterile desert,
Full of red ants as large as elephants and black wasps like pumpkins.
The Five grains don't grow there, only weeds; this is what you will eat
This land dries men out; they seek water without finding any.
You will wander from here or there without ever finding any place to call
    your own in that endless immensity.
Come back, come back! I fear that you will hurl yourself into misfortune!
O soul, come back! The North is no place to stay!
The ice heaped up like mountains, the flying snow that covers a thousand
    leagues.
Come back, come back, You mustn't stay there!
O soul, come back! Don't climb up to the sky!

*Tigers and panthers guard the Nine Portals; they bite and maim the
people from these parts.*
A man with nine heads cuts the tree with nine-thousand branches there
Wolves with piercing eyes come and go
*They hurl people into the air and sport with them, then toss them into a
profound abyss*
In obedience to the orders of the Lord on High and, then, they go to sleep.
Come back, come back! Don't descend to the dark resting place!
The Earth Count with his nine coils, his horns are sharpened
*Thickly muscled and blood dripping claws pursues men there, quickly,
quickly*
He has three eyes and a tiger head and the body of a bull
All these monsters love human flesh
*Come back, come back! I am scared you will throw yourself away in
distress.*

After putting the soul on guard against the dangers that awaited
him in the beyond, the poet who wrote this text invites the soul to
enter into the funerary temple built for him by his family to serve as
his dwelling.

However, in the same way that we who live in a house need to eat
there to sustain ourselves, the soul that now inhabits the ancestral
tablet placed in a temple or a room in the family dwelling has to be
fed. This is done through the offerings made to it by his or her
descendants. If they neglect their duty or the family line is extin-
guished, the soul will suffer from hunger and will perish without a
doubt. One can see, the pains taken to prolong the postmortem
lives of their ancestors are a manifestation of the conscious or unconscious desire felt by people to ensure their own perpetual existence through their descendents.

Despite the variations in Chinese conceptions of the after-death
survival of their relatives, the habit of "feeding" them, in view of

ensuring their survival, is so rooted that Christian missionaries have always experienced the greatest difficulty in getting their converts to renounce it. It is doubtful that they will ever be entirely successful. To renounce the feeding of their dead parents would profoundly offend their feelings of familial piety. If they did so, the majority of Chinese would feel guilty of an assault on the after-death life of those who loved them; they would be guilty of murder.

Also, however long the extended existence of these souls—houen or p'o[9]—can persist following their separation from the body, there is no question of immortality for them. Only their close union with a body that has become immortal could procure eternal life for them.

What steps can be taken to assure oneself of the immortality of a body that everything conspires to show us is destined for destruction? The methods envisioned have many specific details but seem governed by an almost uniform conception of the nature of the body.

The most authoritative of the ancient Taoist authors depict the body under the aspect of a city very similar to Chinese cities, that is to say a city surrounded by ramparts, pierced by gates, flanked by guard towers. This city, that is the body, is not only occupied by the souls discussed in the previous pages but by different gods and the people of their courts. Their dwellings are located along streets and avenues of varying sizes with public squares and crossroads. These dwellings consist of halls, chambers, and pavilions that are always in keeping with their Chinese models. A large retinue of officials and servants keep guard on the city entrances, assure its administrative services, and attend to the various tasks that make

---

9. The houen have the right to the principal worship, but an additional offering is made to the p'o in order to dispel their malign influence that is capable of greatly injuring both the living and their possessions.

up the life of the city. Under the veil of this bizarre topography, initiated Taoist adepts discerned a description of the body's anatomy and the various activities that manifested there and governed its functioning.

The gods—efficient authorities—that the body shelters are both friends and foes to it. The former work to conserve it; the latter work on destroying it. The candidate for immortality must acquire a perfect knowledge of the gods' respective tendencies, their means of action, and their degree of power. He should also clearly discern the location of each one of their dwellings within his body.

The gods residing in the different parts of the body are the same as those inhabiting diverse terrestrial sites—mountains, springs, rivers, and so on. Historians have recounted the astonishment this has provoked among the Taoist faithful in other times. How, people wondered, could a god, who has his palace on that mountain, be found at the same time in the heart or the brain of a human being? To explain this mystery to the naive questioners, theories were built up concerning the faculty of ubiquity that the gods enjoyed.

During these times, within the closed circles of their disciplines, Taoist spiritual masters taught that the inhabitants of our bodies were not at all divine individuals but rather forces, the same as those that are at work in the rock on the mountain peak and the water in the river that flows toward the sea. One law governs the world. All life, which presents itself differently to each of us, is essentially *one*. This very same doctrine is taught today by those rare Taoist teachers that it is still possible to encounter.

The gods that inhabit the body are not fixed to their respective domiciles. They circulate along certain paths that are formed of nerves and veins. It can also happen that certain ones escape or are ejected from the body following struggles with gods of an opposing temperament.

Visitors arriving from the outside and presenting themselves at the gates to the city are either welcomed or find their paths barred at entry by the guards there. One must be vigilant to prevent the entrance of malevolent or dangerous guests. Certain signs such as a buzzing in the ears or sneezing reveal alien presences that are penetrating or trying to penetrate within these ramparts. In these cases, various kinds of practices—the recitation of magic formulas, the ingestion of special pills, or simply a glass of water—are recommended.

The most malefic of these guests are three in number and are known as the three cadavers or the three worms. They install themselves in the body before birth. They have perhaps been incorporated there against its will and without its cooperation in consequence of causes that are difficult to comprehend. These descriptions, which informed Taoists regard as symbolic, have given birth to a number of superstitious practices among the faithful of the working class.

Imprisoned in the body, these worms have the tendency to escape. If successful, they roam at liberty, becoming phantoms and evil spirits. Thus, there is no question of expelling them from the body; they must be destroyed while they are still inside.

These undesirable fellow lodgers are destroyed by following an appropriate diet, consisting primarily of abstaining from grains.[10] These worms are assumed to nourish themselves on grain especially. Some even go so far as to say that they are engendered by grains. Meat, wine, all strong drink, garlic, and onions are also prohibited. This diet must be followed for a great number of years. It is rarely, if ever, used in the present day.

It is only after one has killed the three worms that gnaw on certain bodily organs, with the aid of various dietary abstentions, that

---

10. According to the Chinese: wheat, barley, millet, rice, peas, and beans.

one can begin the superior diet of "feeding on air." This diet consists of assimilating the vital energy in which the world bathes. In this manner one develops "embryonic breathing," which is analogous to the cosmic respiration that gave birth to and sustains the world.

The result of this embryonic breathing is a transformation of the material substance of the body that begins to take effect gradually. The body becomes more subtle, more durable, and finally capable of resisting all causes of destruction.

Embryonic breathing is developed through progressively exercising the capacity to hold one's breath.[11] First, you must know how to breathe deeply—"down to the heels," as the Taoists say. Then, the inhaled air must not remain stationary. It must be made to circulate throughout all the various parts of the body, following a highly detailed itinerary that prescribes the time it should rest in the principal vital centers, located respectively in the brain, the heart, and the lower abdomen.[12] The tissues of the body, traversed by this circulation of air, are imbued with the living fluid that it transports, which they then digest and assimilate. At the same time, the strength of this current carries away the noxious spirits and the enemy gods that have penetrated the body. Thus a new, indestructible body is formed inside the body.

This exercise must be executed under the direction of a competent master; to attempt it without guidance is dangerous. Training should begin at youth. An individual of more than seventy years does not have a chance to manufacture internally those transformations that are necessary to make his body immortal. To even try can be fatal.

---

11. This exercise forms part of Yoga training. We encounter it in all the countries dicussed in this book.

12. These same centers figure in Hindu Yoga where they are called *chakras*.

However, this process can increase one's life span well beyond the normal duration of human life.

The exercises of breath retention should not be practiced at a time or place chosen at random. A high place in the mountains, far removed from human habitation, and in the morning at dawn are indicated as being favorable to these exercises. One must inhale through the nose with the mouth completely shut, whereas one exhales very gently between lips that are clenched, leaving only a slight opening.[13]

Professor Pen Chen, a contemporary Taoist scholar, imparted to me this note concerning the Taoist technical expression "eating breath": "The following quotations are from the *Dialogues of the Patriarch Hwan Yuan Chi*, who lived during the time of the Yuan dynasty (1277–1367). It is not impossible that these discourses may have another master of the same name as their author. Whatever the case may be, the work from which the passage below is taken is very well known in China. It is still kept close at hand by many Taoists who view it as a guide to the spiritual life:

> The breath held in the body or kept outside through the prevention of inhalation is called "primordial breath." It is not nasal breathing. A small portion of this primordial breath is called the embryonic breath in the body, during the beginning stages of Taoist practice. It can be understood as the "cosmic breath,"[14] but Taoists don't make a five-division distinction as do the Indians; they don't regard restrained or held breaths in the same way that the Indians regard *kumbaka*,[15] etc.

---

13. Other methods exist in Tibet and India.
14. The cosmic *prâna*.
15. See the chapter on India.

It is only after the suspension of the physical breath accompanied by the cessation of all mental activity that the embryonic breath will be found in the body. This primordial breath is also called "real breath," "the unique real essence," or "the natural primordial breath." It is without form, without color, without sound, without thought. It is far away and very close.[16] It is neither within nor without. It neither waxes, nor wanes. It is not caused by the satvic activities of man and is consequently "existing"; nor is it caused by the tamasic tendencies and consequently "non-existing."[17] It is the root of all things, previous to creation. Without it nothing could exist.

The awakening of embryonic breathing is the departure point of a movement named "the return to the root" or "the return to life" and taught by Lao-tzu. When this embryonic breathing is set in motion, a feeling of joy fills every cell of the entire body and sends a clear and luminous breath climbing up to the crown of the head in such a way that the senses also become greatly illuminated.[18] Next, this breath dissolves into the spirit, and the Taoist begins his alchemy by preparing the elixir of life within that will make him suitable for immortality.[19]

When speaking of "substance," a distinction is always made between the subtle physical substance and the gross material substance. When Taoists speak of two Heavens, two Earths, and two double Principles, it is clear that these expressions refer to another state of

---

16. We rediscover the language of the Upanishads here.

17. The satvic activities are those directed toward well-being. The tamasic tendencies are those inclined toward inertia and torpor.

18. Here can be found an analogy to the rise of Kundalini-shakti as described in Yoga.

19. This would indicate that the term *alchemy* is employed figuratively by the Taoists and that it is a mistake, committed by many Taoists, to wish it to signify the fabrication of drugs destined to produce immortality.

consciousness (than that of our habitual state). Taoists declare that this other world (perceived in this particular state of awareness) is distinct from our world and yet exists within it. It has a relationship to our world and exercises its influence upon it. It is difficult to completely dismiss a theory that, though often imperfectly and clumsily presented, is nonetheless readily serviceable for practical ends.

When Taoists speak of "eating air" it is as a technical term that means "to avail oneself of," "to make use of." The ordinary meaning of this phrase is "to take within," which causes the ambiguity of the expression "eating air."

"To become immortal" also has another meaning in Taoism. This expression doesn't necessarily mean a very long physical existence, even though this is a possibility contained and concealed in this expression. The principal signification is "to unite oneself with the 'Eternal Principle' and consequently elevate oneself above nature." Abilities such as being able to withdraw oneself at will within a body or to expand like breath itself or to possess the capability of projecting countless emanations are also included in the definition of immortality.

There are no special rules concerning the propitious moments to practice respiratory exercises, but there are precautions that should be taken. If these moments are understood to mean the twelve divisions of night and day, several directions are supplied. If it concerns personal dispositions or favorable or unfavorable outside conditions, then certain other indications are present. If it is a question of the ups and downs that will be inevitably experienced during the course of a very long Taoist practice, or even if it concerns a critical moment or the primary importance of the practice itself, then these will again be different. Whatever the case may be, certain things will become naturally and spontaneously evident to those who are spiritually qualified in this regard and have made themselves capable of perceiving them.

Works of Taoist inspiration that deal with primordial breath or mind are numerous. Here is an extract from one of them entitled *The Secret of the Golden Flower*.[20] This book belongs to a treasury of esoteric writings generally considered to contain the oral teachings that have been handed down by master to disciple in China since times of great antiquity. *The Secret of the Golden Flower* is assumed to have been published in the eighth century A.D. It discusses an energy figuratively called the "Golden Flower" or "Elixir of Life," which must be created and then made to circulate throughout the body.

This teaching is attributed to Lu Yen, who would have received it from a disciple who had received it directly from Lao-tzu. Numerous legends have been woven around the personality of Lu Yen. He is represented as being one of the Immortals. Several other masters are recognized as having subscribed to theories analogous to those presented by Lu Yen.

Like all works of its kind, *The Secret of the Golden Flower* has been crafted in a language of obscurity. This obscurity may have been desired by the author, who wished the reading of his work to be reserved to a small circle of students for whom the theories he presented were already somewhat familiar. But neither is it doubtful that these theories, which rest on particular states of consciousness, would be impossible to explain verbally to those who hadn't at least started the practice of Taoist exercises. Generally, Taoists believe that the explanations provided by a master who is familiar with the language of the doctrines are almost indispensable to the reader.

The Master Lao-tzu said:

> That which exists by itself is called Tao. The Tao has neither name nor form. It is the unique essence and the primal mind.

---

20. For more information on this text consult the commentaries of Professor C. G. Jung in *The Secret of the Golden Flower*.

Essence and Life cannot be seen. They are contained in the Celestial Light.

I am going to reveal to you the secret of the Golden Flower of the Great One. The Great One is the name given to that above which there is nothing. The magic of life consists of using action to achieve non-action.[21] The intermediary steps must not be neglected by those desiring to enter directly into the secret.

The precepts that have been handed down invite us to undertake work upon the essence with no delay. But in so doing we must be on our guard to avoid taking the wrong path.

The Golden Flower is Light. This term serves as a figurative expression to designate the truly transcendent power of the *Great One*.

If an individual attains this One, he becomes alive, if he fails, he dies. But, even if an individual dwells in the power (the cosmic breath or respiration), he doesn't necessarily perceive it, in the same manner that fish don't see the water even though they live in it. An individual dies for want of vital breath just as fish will perish if they are taken out of the water. For this reason, the initated masters have taught us to attach ourselves to the primordial and to guard the One, which is the circulation of the Light. By protecting one's veritable power one can prolong the duration of one's life and then concentrate on putting the method of creating an immortal body into action.

Consequently, all one has to do is make the Light circulate; this is the most profound and marvelous of secrets. If the Light is permitted to circulate for a sufficient length of time in a circle it will solidify. At this point it is the natural spiritual body.

This is the condition that has been described in the book of the

---

21. The doctrine of non-action is also taught in Tibet.

seal of the heart as follows: "Silently you will soar on high." Following this method will preclude the need to follow any other. All that is necessary is to concentrate your thought upon it. It is also said: "By concentrating your thoughts you can fly and be reborn in Heaven." Heaven is not the immense blue vault above, in this case, but rather the place where the body is constructed at the site of the creative power. If this method is followed with persistence one will naturally develop, another spiritual body in addition to the material body.

The Golden Flower is the Elixir of Life. All modifications of spiritual consciousness depend on the heart.[22] There is a secret kind of sorcery here that, even though it produces its effect in a highly precise manner, is so subtle that it requires a high degree of intelligence and perspicacity as well as a perfect calm and concentration to make use of it. Those who are not provided with that kind of intelligence and high degree of understanding will not succeed in discovering the means to make use of this charm. Those who do not possess the most perfect capability to concentrate their mind and establish a total state of serenity will be incapable of grasping it.[23]

---

22. One should take precaution to not take these terms—*heart, flower, elixir,* and others—in their literal sense. These are symbolic expressions. The *heart* is the center, the base; *elixir* is a current of energy and so on. However, this text distinguishes between two coexisting principles—one that is natural and physical, the other of subtle or spiritual essence. Here we encounter again the theory of two souls, or two *Is* and, indirectly, that of the body and its subtle double.

23. The commentary says: "If a man succeeds in being perfectly calm, the Celestial Heart will manifest of its own accord. When sensation rises and overflows by following its natural inclination, the individual is created as the primordial individual. Between the moment of conception and that of birth, this individual dwells in veritable space. It is at birth that the idea of individuality looms up, essence and life are split in half. If an absolute calmness is not achieved they will remain unreconciled."

◆ ◆ ◆

The Master Lao-tzu said, "If one were to compare him to Heaven and Earth, man would be less than a fly, but compared to sense, the Tao, Heaven and Earth are less than a water bubble, less than a shadow. Only the Primal Mind, the true Essence, surpasses both time and space."

The power of the seed, like Heaven and Earth, is subject to death but the Primal Mind is situated beyond these two opposing polarities.[24]

When the student learns to grasp the Primal Mind, he triumphs over the contrasts of light and darkness. He no longer lingers in the three worlds. But only he or she who has contemplated essence in its original manifestation is capable of doing this.

When the human being leaves the womb, the primal mind dwells in the little spot located between the eyes, but the conscious spirit resides beneath the heart. This heart is dependent upon the outside world.

If a man goes without eating for even a single day he feels bad. If he hears something frightening he trembles, if he contemplates death he becomes saddened. But the Celestial Heart placed in the head remains unaffected. It is not good for it to be moved or affected by anything.

When the common man dies, his mind is moved; this is not a good occurrence. It is better that the Light has been already strengthened in a spiritual body and the vital forces have gradually penetrated one's instincts and movements. This is a secret that has not been revealed for thousands of years.

The inferior or lower heart moves like a powerful chief who scorns the Celestial Chief because it is weak and replaces him as head of

---

24. Beginning and end.

state. But when the primordial castle can be fortified and defended, it is as if a wise and strong chieftain were sitting on the throne. The right and left eyes put the light into circulation like two ministers who assist the chieftain with all their strength. When this chieftain, who is in the middle, is in good order, all the quarrelsome warriors submit to him and accept his orders.

Immortality is not Eternity. The Taoist Immortal can hope to endure, at most, for as long as the world. A time will come when this world—with its gods, its lands, the stars, and all its constituent elements—will disintegrate and be engulfed by the Chaos from which it has emerged.[25] The dream of immortality for this Immortal will be ended; it will vanish just like the dream of a single night with no dreamer remaining to remember it.

Taoism does not attain its objective with physical immortality. It has not resolved the problem of an infinite existence. The majority of its adepts, without renouncing its ritual practices—especially those dependent on magic and sorcery—have turned to Buddhism and the different doctrines that entered China in its wake.

Currently, the majority of Chinese possess a belief in reincarnation similar to that of Indians,[26] that is to say a belief in an immaterial personal principle[27] that leaves the body of the dying. The reward or punishment that the departed has earned by his deeds is experienced as sojourns of varying lengths of time in pleasant or painful extraterrestrial locations. The deceased then reincarnates and takes a place in our world again.

---

25. The Indians believe in the dissolution and disintegration of the world, which they refer to as *pralâya*.

26. The materialist or agnostic Confucians are an exception.

27. This plays the role of the soul.

While the majority of Taoists followed this path, a small elite returned to the original teachings, or perhaps they never truly abandoned them. These individuals didn't seek immortality; they felt they were eternal. Thus, where the candidates for a material immortality fed their bodies, these adepts sought to nourish their spirits. They set a corporeal dietary regimen, which they retained for its hygienic value, in opposition to the practice of contemplative meditation.

The fundamental doctrine of Taoism is that of *non-action*. This is what is most plainly exhibited in the Tao Te Ching and the teachings based on that work. "Tao Te Ching" is translated as "the book of the Tao" and "Tao" is, literally, "the Way," which in its Chinese significance, is the "Beingness"[28] analogous to the Brahmin of the Indian Vedanta. The Tao Te Ching is attributed to Lao-tzu, a personage that emerges from a thick veil of legend and of whom, in fact, we know nothing, except that ancient Chinese authors refer to him as having lived around the sixth century B.C.

According to tradition, the sage Lao-tzu, seen by some as an Immortal who reached an immense age, decided to leave China for the "Country of the West," in other words, Tibet. Mounted on an ox, he wandered across the territory of the extreme northwest of China, which today is the province of Kansu.[29]

---

28. "Beingness" [English in the original. *Trans.*], not *a* being but "the *state* of being" par excellence.

29. I have traveled this same route thinking of Lao-tzu. It doesn't really matter whether or not he really existed; his legend has been repeated across the centuries, and the doctrine that is attributed to him has created a mental personality that is more alive than the colorless personalities of the majority of men. Wouldn't this be the true immortality? I believe I have spotted him myself, wandering in front of me and disappearing into the distance, losing himself in that country of eternal mystery—Tibet.

When Lao-tzu arrived at the fort guarding the Chinese frontier, the official residing there asked him before quitting China to leave a book that would perpetuate his teaching[30] and preserve, for the benefit of generations to come, the memory of the truths, which had appeared to him during the course of his meditations. Acceding to his request, the sage stopped there for several days and wrote the Tao Te Ching, then continued on into the west and was never seen again. Whatever historical facts may be hidden beneath this tradition, Lao-tzu founded a school by means of this Tao Te Ching.

It is not certain whether the doctrine of non-action preached by Lao-tzu was a personal innovation. It seems that the Chinese have always tended to believe that the natural play of things rules their behavior without the administrative presence of any outside power. If man interferes in this natural order, if he claims to bring change or improvements to it, he disturbs it and a fatal disorder results. As this was the case in regard to the physical world—the succession of the seasons, the tides, the movements of the stars, and so on—the Taoists extended the same conception to the plane of mental activity. The mind should be left in its natural state. It shouldn't be disturbed with conflicting thoughts and the construction of ideas and so forth.

This is what Taoist non-action consists of.[31] One mustn't be fooled into thinking the expression "non-action" means that those who practice it cease all material activity and embrace inertia; that is not it at all. The Taoist attends to his normal occupations and to those intellectual and material situations in which he finds himself, but his mental attitude is different from that of the individual who

---

30. He never wrote anything.

31. There are close analogies to this among those Buddhists who preach the suppression of *samskâras* and among the orthodox adepts of Pantanjâli Yoga.

believes he controls the flow of events that concern him or from those people who take on the coloring of the environment in which they find themselves. He understands that he doesn't control the course of life any more than the stars consciously control their revolutions or the seasons rule their progression. He understands that he is a participant in the eternal and inconceivable Life of the Tao and that, like Existence itself, he is eternal motion, without doing anything.

The Taoist meditation is a non-meditation. It doesn't propose any subject or investigation on which to focus. It even pushes away any naturally occurring thoughts that may come to the meditator once he enters a life of contemplation. He is content to let his intellect unfold effortlessly, just as the body functions with no need for him to direct his heartbeat or the respective tasks of his internal organs.

Later in this practice, no thought—thought creates a duality: the thinker and the thing thought—will emerge in a mind that has become like a polished mirror, a still lake with no banks to limit its expansion. Nothing breaks the surface of its waters, which reflect an infinite, cloudless sky.

However, the Taoist, like all other mystics, is inclined to be aware of his diffusion into the Supreme Unity; and if he is aware of it, then it is a sign of his imperfection. The sense of rapture that persists in the ecstatic state is a demonstration of this imperfection. Thus, even as all apparent physical activity has ceased and the body has become insensitive, the feeling of duality persists in the lower depths of the mind of the individual who experiences the spiritual voluptuousness of contact with the Tao, Brahman, or God. They still remain an *Other* to him or her.

A true integral union would inevitably lead to a total lack of awareness of one's self and, perhaps, to death.

The state of voluptuousness that appears supramaterial to some adepts is a snare into which countless Taoists have stepped. They have sought to achieve it through the use of drugs or even the simple intoxication produced by wine as others elsewhere have found it through the aid of music or incense.

Nothing is easier or more ordinary than to fool oneself while seeking spiritual union and to believe erroneously and pridefully that one has ascended to supernormal levels of consciousness; whereas in reality, one has become bogged down in a series of fruitless ramblings and sensations that have more to do with pathology than spirituality.

"To seek" union with the Tao, with the Whole, with the One denotes a total lack of understanding. This union cannot be produced: it exists, it has always existed.

"What did your face look like before your mother and father were born?" is a problem (koan) that Zen[32] masters have posed for centuries to their disciples. This face is no different from the one I wear today. This is what is to be understood, what is to be *seen*. I don't have to "make myself immortal." The Eternal *is*, simultaneously unity and diversity, *me* and the *other*; the Tao. The Tao, which is the supreme immutability, creates everything by doing nothing.

---

32. Ts'an, which is Zen in Japanese, has borrowed much from Taoism.

TIBET

THE THEORIES THAT WE ENCOUNTER IN TIBET CONCERNING LIFE after death and related subjects are not completely foreign to the West. We do not lack for people among us who are inclined to believe in reincarnation, or even those who believe in it wholeheartedly. Others assert the existence of disembodied spirits or of a subtle "double" of the body that is not destroyed by death. Tibet—a crossroads where immigrants from all four corners of the globe and even, according to certain legends, extraterrestrial regions, have met and mingled together—offers a remarkable diversity of these beliefs. Each group of immigrants brought with them their own conceptions concerning the capital subject of the universally desired, limitless perpetuation of individual existence.

Tibetans are generally considered to be Buddhists. Indeed they are, but in varying degrees and styles. It is especially true that they believe themselves to be Buddhists—and the only authentic Buddhists in the whole world, at that. So strong are they in that conviction that they obstinately regard their fellow Buddhists throughout Asia with either scorn or pity.[1] Certainly, they concede, we owe

---

1. The *Théravadins* (disciples of the ancients) are known in the West as *Hinayâna* (adepts of the small vehicle). In Tibetan, tchég chung or tchég men *(thég dmen)*

much to the learned teachers of India. This fact is recognized on a daily basis since several morsels of food are offered before every meal along with the following formula: "The pundits of India have shown themselves to be favorably disposed toward Tibet."

It is true, Tibetans admit, that once upon a time, a long time ago, certain lamas did go to be instructed in the doctrine of Buddha, in the great Buddhist colleges of India, at Nalanda and elsewhere, and that they brought back with them and translated into their own language a quantity of works by Indian masters of the doctrine. The doctrine that they introduced to Tibet is now preserved there because it was forgotten by the Indians.[2] Thus, the Tibetans have proudly attributed to their land the exclusive title "Homeland of Religion,"[3] formerly bestowed on India, the native land of Buddha.

Buddhists share a unanimous belief in reincarnation even though that doctrine doesn't expressly figure—quite the contrary—in the first teaching that is regarded to have been proclaimed directly by the Buddha Siddhartha Guatama.[4] Since the Tibetans accept reincarnation in principle, what form do they imagine it takes? There is quite an abundant and varied number of forms in theory as well as in practice. But first of all one point must be understood. Just what is it that is reincarnated? According to the most common idea it is the *namshés*.

---

means inferior vehicle. The term *thég pa* signifies a religious doctrine, a rule of conduct which like a vehicle transports one to an objective, spiritual salvation.

2. It is true that a number of Buddhist works written in Sanskrit have been lost in India over the course of wars and persecutions mounted against the Buddhists. Previously they had been translated into Tibetan, and these translations have been rediscovered in the libraries of various monasteries.

3. *Tcheu kyi yul (chos kyi yul).*

4. We will return to this subject further on.

The term *namshés* is an abbreviated form of *namparshéspa.*[5] It is the name of a principle that "knows," one that takes into account the objects that our senses have entered into contact with and differentiates and classifies them. There are six distinct namparshéspa. Each of the five senses has its own particular namparshéspa.[6] A sixth namparshéspa is attached to the mind.[7] It is regarded as the awareness of the personality, that which has an idea of the *I.*

However, the Tibetan masses have made the namshés into the equivalent of the Indian *jîva,* which plays a similar role.[8] The namshés is a spiritual entity attached to the material body but not entirely dependent upon it, which separates from it at the time of death and ceases to be usable by it. This namshés will then emigrate and take up residence in another body, "like one takes off a worn garment to put on another" (Bhagavad Gîtâ).

The namshés is not free, however, to choose the new body of its choice to live in. This decision is imposed on it by the automatic play of cause and effect—the "game of action" *(karma).* The causes

---

5. *Nam par shés pa (rnampar shéspa)* the "knower of all"; *vijâna* in Sanskrit.

6. *Mig kyi namparshéspa,* awareness resulting from sight or resulting from sight by means of the eye *(mig).* And so on, awareness of sound associated with the ear, etc. Namparshéspa is one of the constituent elements of the individual.

7. *Yid ki* namparshéspa. *Yid* = Sanskrit *manas.* The Tibetans have three words for designating the mind. *Yid* is most particularly the intellectual faculty, the power of perception, and the imagination. *Lo (blo)* is the affective faculty, the natural dispositions; these are equivalent to the Sanskrit terms *Buddha, prajnâ. Séms* has a vast expanse of meanings, it is the translation of the Sanskrit terms *citta, manas,* and also *satva.* In polite language these three terms are referred to as *thugs.*

8. This *jîva* shouldn't be considered the equivalent of the soul spoken of in Western religions. It is not created for each individual in particular at the moment of birth.

that determine the nature of its reincarnation are the acts[9] that it has accomplished through the intermediary of the individual with whom it has been united in course of several past lives.

No supreme power governs the reincarnation of the jîva namshés. The latter is automatically led toward the new body it must inhabit. This new body is not strange to it in the same manner that an article of clothing bought in a store is initially strange to the person who puts it on. It is the namshés itself which has, in the course of its union with the material body, woven and styled the garment that is found ready to wear.

This process of "confection" is continuous. From time to time the namshés tailor does some retouching on work done previously. It modifies the aspect of the garment by adding different pieces of cloth to it or by covering it with ornaments that incorporate themselves into the fabric and transform it. The incessant activity of the body, mind, and spirit[10] is depicted as manufacturing the individual destiny that it pursues from reincarnation to reincarnation through the succession of birth and death. Only the ignorant speak of punishment and reward. There is only the sovereign and inexorably rational law of cause and effect or, as the Tibetans say, "the act and its fruits."

Numerous fantasies have been spun on the theme of reincarnation. A judge of the dead has been imagined.[11] However, the Tibet-

---

9. Works accomplished by either the body, the word, or the mind (thoughts, desires, etc.).

10. The spirit isn't an "individual" distinct from the body that plays the role of its companion. This is what differentiates it from the idea of soul as conceived by westerners. The spirit depends on the body for its existence. There is no "mentality" separate from sensations, the perceptions formed by the senses. The ancient Indian masters said earlier: "The spirit, the mind is food" (Chandogya Upanishad).

11. *Shindjé*, the *Yâma* of the Indians. India, China, and the Western religions also all have the appearance of the souls before a judge.

ans have not attributed to this judge the ability to evaluate the merits and demerits of the dead that present themselves before him. He is not qualified to pronounce sentence upon them after he has weighed his judgment. The acts of the deceased touch him in no way whatsoever; he feels neither benevolence nor animosity toward them. His role consists only of announcing to them the fate that their own actions have prepared for them.

Sometimes this judge informs himself about the good and bad deeds of the deceased by consulting an ever up-to-date account book. Sometimes these actions are represented by white and black pebbles placed on the trays of a pair of scales. The result of this weighing indicates what sentence to hand down.

Another picturesque fantasy features a coatroom within this courtroom in which are hung the skins of different kinds of men and animals. The namshés automatically re-clothes itself in one of these skins, which indicates the fate that has been reserved for it. It can become a goat, a horse, or a bird; it can become humpbacked, sickly or handsome, male or female.

Yet another of these fantastic conceptions concerning life after death has two roads leading from this courtroom. One of these roads leads down toward the worlds ruled by suffering—the various hells—the other climbs toward the different paradises.

But consistent throughout these widely differing fantasies is the theme that no arbitrary decision governs the fate of the namshés. It is fitting to note here that neither the agreeable or disagreeable conditions toward which the namshés directs itself is definitive. The new life it enters will always end and give way to another that is capable of being quite different from the one previous.[12] One dies

---

12. Generally, all the effects of the actions achieved in one incarnation neither manifest themselves nor are fully exhausted in the following incarnation. These effects that are "held in reserve" can combine themselves with those emanating from the immediately preceding incarnation. The law of cause and effect doesn't

in hell just as one dies in paradise. One will die in the six classes of being.[13] The Tibetans neither believe in eternal bliss nor accept the horror of an eternal hell.

The effects that have been engendered by causes that are temporally produced (acts of a limited duration) are incapable of having an infinite scope and lasting eternally; their efficiency is used up. The effects that our actions have brought about are also worn out in the same way. However, this "wear and tear" cannot be produced in the space of a single lifetime. A remaining balance of effects that have not been worn out can be carried over into another incarnation and there combine with effects derived from the activities of the new incarnation. Countless theories have been elaborated on just this subject.

Also to be noted here is the theory concerning actions producing no results that would affect the nature of the following incarnation: these are "sterile" actions. According to this theory, these are actions governed by causes belonging to a previous life, actions which are "results" that have not sprung forth by conscious will. These purely mechanical manifestations can be somewhat assimilated into the personality as reflex movements.

However, certain Tibetans don't accept the existence of these sterile actions. They object that this theory is based on a moral conception of karma as an agent of retribution for the "good" and "bad" acts

---

consist of simple, straight lines, but rather is made up of combinations and entanglements that, even though not deviating from the initial principle, will result in effects that were quite unforeseen. It should be noted that an effect is never the product of one cause but rather the combination of several. Moreover, the principal cause only comes into play in association with secondary causes: physical and mental ambiance, and so on.

13. The gods, the non-gods (a kind of titan), men, non-men (genies, fairies, etc.), animals, the inhabitants of the worlds of suffering.

accomplished by a particular individual and not solely as an impersonal succession of activities that are undistinguished from their moral value. Every action, these latter say, ineluctably produces effects that are both great and small, occurring both soon or after a long delay, and are either apparent or remain imperceptible to the individual in question. *The world is movement.*

We can come close to this theory of sterile actions with two relative conceptions concerning the fate of the deceased. Both of these conceptions belong to a somewhat elevated degree of the Tibetan religion. According to one of these theories, the man who has prepared the conditions of his future life during this life will passively undergo the effects of his past actions in this new incarnation until their effects have been totally exhausted with nothing added to them by the activity that unfolds in the situation in which he has been placed. Thus, the fortunate who are reborn in a paradise taste there the joys available to its inhabitants; the unfortunate who have prepared for themselves a place in whatever hell or lower world, that of the animals and so forth, will undergo the sufferings that are proper to these worlds; but in this state they can have no influence on the condition that will fall due to them in a future life. However, according to a different conception, the feelings and the will remain active—even though at varying degrees of strength—among the inhabitants of all the worlds, and these feelings and the will are susceptible to producing effects not only in the following life but even in their current life.

There are countless tales that illustrate this belief. Here is one of the most popular in Tibet:

> Because of the abominable acts he had committed, a criminal was reborn in a hell in the form of a horse. As such he was harnessed with two other horses to a very heavy carriage. The torture inflicted upon these unfortunates consisted of pulling this carriage

up an incredibly steep path to the top of a mountain. Despite their conjoined efforts, the three animals were unsuccessful at moving this heavy vehicle and the demons whipped them mercilessly. Then a huge wave of compassion surged up in the heart of the ex-criminal-turned-horse-in-hell.

"Detach my companions," he said to his torturers, "free them, I will pull the carriage by myself."

"Miserable animal," cried one of the demons in fury, "you cannot even budge this carriage as three, how dare you claim to be able to do it all alone."

And in a fit of rage, the demon hammered a terrible blow with the iron stock of his whip onto the skull of the compassionate horse. The latter fell down dead and was immediately reborn in paradise.

We know that Buddhism considers compassion the most important of all the virtues. By altering the mentality of the ex-criminal, it transported him to a corresponding plane of existence. As the common people of Tibet say, he has been rewarded for his charitable thought. As it is understood by more learned Tibetans, he had transformed his mental state, and it is the mental state that automatically places an individual in its corresponding milieu.

We will now examine a process of reincarnation described in a very detailed fashion in the works entitled Bardo Thödal (Bardo Thos grol). A certain number of versions of this work exists that are identical in regard to their objective, even though different in their details. Bardo Thödal signifies "a text that when heard provides delivery from the Bardo." The Bardo is the intermediary state that the disincarnated soul remains in from the moment of death until reincarnation.

The original Sanskrit text that served as a base for the various versions currently existing has been lost, if indeed it ever existed, which is probable but not absolutely certain. This Bardo Thödal forms part of the *tér* or *térma* (*gter*, which means treasures). Those writings denoted as *tér* are those that their author, Padmasambhava,[14] had buried or hidden in different locations because he deemed the Tibetans of his epoch incapable of understanding their meaning, and he wished to reserve the privilege of reading them for more intellectually developed future generations. From time to time, a lama or a layperson boasts of having found one of these writings, but the *tertöns* (*gter ston*, discoverers of treasures), though numerous in past centuries, have become increasingly rare, and the works that are considered "recuperated" form a foundation (around fifty books) to which any addition no longer seems permissible.

Do the theories exposed in the Bardo Thödal represent conceptions that are purely and exclusively Indian? There is reason to doubt it. The different Bardo Thödal doctrines offer, as a matter of fact,

---

14. Padmasambhava was originally from Oudiana, a region that today forms part of Afghanistan. He didn't belong to the Buddhist religious order (the *sangha*). He was married. He was a savant adept of Tantra, famous for its magical powers. He was, for a time, a professor at the renowned university of Nalanda.

The Tibetan king Tisrong De Tsen (Kri srong Dé Tsan) had undertaken the construction of a large monastery at Samye, which had not been achieved because the local demons demolished each night all the work accomplished by the workers on the previous day. On the recommendation of Santarakishta, his Indian chaplain and the brother-in-law of Padmasambhava, the king invited the latter to Tibet to exercise his occult powers against the demons of Samye. Padmasambhava arrived in Tibet in 747 and vanquished the demons, who from that point instead of demolishing the work done by the builders did it themselves with a miraculous rapidity. It was Padmasambhava who introduced Tantricism to Tibet, where it was incorporated into Buddhism. Padmasambhava means "born of the lotus." According to legend, Padmasambhava appeared miraculously in a lotus in the center of a lake. The Tibetans named him Guru Rinpoche (the Precious Master) or Guru Péma (Master Lotus) or Ougyen Péma (Lotus of Ougyen, Ougyen for Oudiana).

similarities on more than one point with doctrines belonging to the ancient pre-Buddhist religion of Tibet, the *Bön*, which was similar to Taoism.

However, there is no point in discussing the origins of the Bardo Thödal but rather in presenting the reincarnation process it describes. It matters little who conceived it; it is a product of human thought pursuing its untiring desire for individual perpetuity.

The Bardo Thödal claims to teach those who have not attained Buddhist salvation during the course of their terrestrial lives the means to succeed in doing so after their death. Buddhist salvation consists of freeing oneself from the chain of deaths and successive rebirths: the "wheel," which in Sanskrit is *samsâra*. This liberation is produced by the ascension to awareness, to the spiritual illumination that dissipates the dream, rich in suffering, in which we live, prisoners of the creations of our own imaginations.

At times the Bardo Thödal is studied under the direction of a competent master, and those who dedicate themselves to that study are assumed to know what awaits them after their death. They are even regarded as capable of directing it in a fashion that will be satisfying for them. For others, that is to say, the great majority of people, the Bardo Thödal fills the role of a "traveler's guide" to the beyond.

For the common Tibetan, the Bardo Thödal has almost entirely lost the character of a guide to the beyond. The lamas who chant it rarely understand the words they are pronouncing. For them there is nothing more to it than a series of rhythmically chanted syllables; and most of the time they are of the same opinion as the relatives of the deceased, who attribute this reading with the magical power of transferring the namshés of the dead person, near whom the book is read, to the Western Paradise of the Great Beatitude (*Noub Déwa chén*). The same result is expected in regard to any individual who has recently died. A rite called *powa*—associated with the reading of the Bardo Thödal or practiced even more briefly on its own—is also regarded as an appropriate means for transferring the namshés to the Western Paradise.

All Tibetans believe that death is the beginning of an arduous and perilous journey that an individual must execute within the interval of time before their next reincarnation into one or another of the six categories. Reincarnation is the end of the journey.

The regions the deceased will have to travel are described to him during this reading, and they are closely modeled on the countryside that is familiar to the Tibetans. He will have to scale high mountains along steep paths, ford large and fast-moving rivers, and traverse arid, desert regions where, as elsewhere, both demons and brigands are on the lookout. May he not forget to ask protection from Dolma, the Guardian of travelers. . . .

As befits a practical people, the Tibetans possess the charitable impulse to strengthen the dying or recently deceased individuals for the rigorous journey about to be undertaken. Accordingly, he will be served a meal several times a day as long as he is still in residence at his house while waiting for the day of the funeral.

The period that elapses between the time of death and the funeral is always a long one. To shorten it would appear to show a lack of respect for the dead, as if one was in a hurry to be rid of him. It is also suitable, in a country where the villages are as far apart as they are in Tibet, to give the invited guests the time necessary to travel a distance of one hundred to one hundred fifty miles or more over difficult mountain roads. The greater the number of people attending the funeral, the greater the honor shown to the deceased in the eyes of the family. The honor thus shown quite naturally extends to all of his or her relatives.

The corpses of eminent personalities, such as the great lamas, are embalmed or mummified by being immersed in salt. The corpse of the latest Pentchen Lama, who died in Chinese territory when about to return to Tibet,[15] was preserved in this manner. Each day the salt that had become moist was replaced by fresh salt, and the used salt that had become imbued with the fluid emanating from the cadaver was then sold to the devout who used it as a medication.

Another way of preserving the corpse of a great lama was to plunge it into a vat of boiling butter. Next, the face of the mummy was gilded and its body dressed. The mummy could then remain displayed in a glass case. These mummies are called *mardong* (butter figures).

The majority of the dead are dressed in their most beautiful clothing. Instead of being laced together as normally would be the case, the clothes are put on the body backward. This appears to be a means of informing the deceased that they no longer belong in the world of the living, a fact that they don't always understand.

The body is seated and then held in that position with scarves that are tied together. A cooking pot or other large receptacle, covered with drapery, serves as a seat for the cadaver. This receptacle is filled with grain to absorb the fluids caused by the putrefaction of the body and prevent them from overflowing. If the exhibit of the body is extended over a long period of time, then the dampened grain is replaced with fresh grain.

As is the case with the salt, this grain is never discarded; but in the case of an ordinary Tibetan, it is not supposed to have gained

---

15. The late Dalai Lama had accused the Pentchen of Chinese sympathies and planned to lure him to Lhasa where he would then be imprisoned. The Pentchen, in fear for his life, fled to China, where he was held in great esteem. There he remained for several years. After the death of the Dalai Lama, his persecutor, he was returning to his fief, the Tsang province of Tibet. I was in Tibet, on the Chinese border, when these events transpired.

any special qualities from being used in this fashion. It is just washed, given to animals, or quite simply used like any other grain.

My adopted son, Yongden, who as a young Lama had often attended or participated in these renowned rituals during the long period preceding a funeral, told me that the odor of putrefaction emanating from the corpse was oftentimes abominable. However, the officiating priests never appeared to exhibit any discomfort and greeted the festive meals they were served with a hearty appetite. Their host, the deceased, was often encouraged to imitate them and to eat his fill, while he still had the chance.

It is in the superstitious atmosphere that fills the majority of Tibetan homes that the Bardo Thödal is read—a symbolic poem, written by the learned for the learned, that serves even today as a theme for study and meditation among certain thinkers of this high "country of the snows."[16]

---

16. *Khams yul*: the country of the snows is the name that Tibetans give to their land even though, singularly enough, it hardly ever snows in Tibet except on the highest mountain peaks.

THE BARDO THÖDAL

HAVE YOU RECEIVED THE TEACHING OF A WISE MASTER
initiated into the mysteries of the Bardo?[1]

If you have received it, recall it to your memory and don't allow
yourself to be distracted by any other thoughts.

If it is the spiritual master of the dying person who is in attendance, then he says:

> I have transmitted to you the profound teaching that I myself
> received from my master and, through him, from a long line of
> initiated gurus.
>
> Recall it to your memory and don't allow yourself to be dis-
> tracted by any other thoughts.

I. Let's repeat that Bardo means "going between two," that is to say, between
death and a new rebirth. The objective of reading this text next to an individual
who is dying is to enlighten him or her on what to expect after expiring: the
"mental" voyage they will accomplish and the possibilities that will become available to them of achieving liberation from the wheel of successive rebirths or, in
default of that, how to procure a rebirth in happier circumstances. If this possibility has been unavailable during the life that is about to end, it can still be found in
the state that is entered following death.

Steadfastly maintain your mental lucidity.

If you are suffering, do not allow yourself to be absorbed by the sensations caused by your suffering.

If you feel a restful torpor invade your mind,

If you feel yourself sinking into a calm darkness, a pacifying oblivion,

Don't surrender to it. Remain alert.

The consciousnesses,[2] which have been known as the being N. [the name of the person being addressed by the Lama], have a tendency to disperse. Retain them with the strength of the *Yid kyi namparshéspa*.

Your consciousnesses are separating from your body and entering the Bardo.

Appeal to your energy to allow you to see them as you cross the threshold and retain total consciousness.

The vivid clarity of the Light without color and emptiness will appear and envelop you with a quickness greater than lightning.

Don't allow fear to make you retreat and lose consciousness. Plunge into that light.

Reject all belief in an ego and all attachment to your illusionary personality.

Dissolve its Non-being into Being and be free.

There are very few individuals who, having lacked the capability to attain liberation during their lifetime, can do so at this moment

---

2. The five consciousnesses are attached to each of the five senses respectively, and mental consciousness, considered in Buddhism a sixth sense with ideas as its organ, is the *Yid Kyi namparshéspa*. It is also self-awareness, the consciousness one has of being a personality, an *I*. This is regarded as a mistaken impression.

that is so fleeting that it can be said to be without duration. Others, affected by the fear that is experienced as a fatal shock, lose consciousness.

At the moment the dying individual expires, the lama in attendance—if he has been initiated into this practice and has received the power to execute it effectively—blurts out "hick!" three times followed by a single shout of "phet!" Next he continues, or if called upon to recite in the company of someone already dead,[3] he begins here:

One such as you [name of the deceased] will reawaken as if from sleep
Know that you have abandoned the body you animated.
Look at it, it lies there inert.
Don't feel any regret.
Don't feel any form of attachment for it.
Don't linger around those who have been your friends and family.
Don't strive to speak to them.
Your voice makes no sound; they cannot hear it.
Don't linger to traverse your fields, to contemplate the things that had
* belonged to you.*
You do not have the power to move them and carry them away.
You have left them behind.

---

3. It can also occur, when the real corpse is absent, but has been deceased for no more than several days, that the Bardo Thödal ritual is read in the presence of a mannequin clad in the deceased's clothes. This is patently illogical because if the consciousness of the individual has already traveled into the Bardo, no one can know with any certainty how far he has progressed, and the advice thus given him could concern a stage other than the one he finds himself in. The forty-nine days that current belief assigns to the duration of the Bardo journey are as symbolical as the six days of Creation. Educated lamas declare that these pilgrimages in the Bardo are achieved in a time that is dependent upon the mental state of the traveler.

They have left you.

Don't feel any attachment to them.

Don't seek to renew the ties that bound you to them.

Detach yourself.

Know that you have created a dream that was furnished by forms without consistency. Since you did not seize the Liberation at the moment when Light-Reality enveloped, you will continue to drift through pleasant and unpleasant dreams. In the course of these dreams you will be offered opportunities of attaining Awareness.

Remain vigilant, remain alert.

Now understand this: each of the consciousnesses, which together formed your personality by virtue of your physical organs whose material is going to dissolve, will continue its particular activity until it has totally exhausted the energy engendered by the past actions that keep it in activity.

It's by virtue of the past activity of your mind and body that the visions surrounding you appear.

Because awareness of forms and colors has come through your eyes, you see forms and colors.

Because awareness of sounds has come to you through your ears, you hear sounds.

Because awareness of odors has come to you through your nose, you smell odors.

Because awareness of flavors has come through your tongue, you taste flavors.

Because awareness of tactile sensations has come through your body, you feel tactile sensations.

Because your mind has manufactured ideas derived from these awarenesses, ideas come to you.

Know that in this place these are nothing but hallucinations.

None of the things offered to you are real.

They are the products of your past awarenesses.

Don't be scared by them.

Don't become attached to them.

Contemplate them with indifference, without aversion or desire.

If the thoughts and charitable acts, the patience, the effort expended in pursuit of Good and mental tranquillity[4] have been predominant in your past life, if at the moment of your death you made vows of compassion for the good of all beings, and if your aspirations are directed toward the Buddhas and Bodhisattvas, with the desire of approaching them and becoming one with their beneficial activity, then the Buddhas and Bodhisattvas will appear in radiant form to you surrounded by an infinitely luminous clear blue light.

Despite their sweetness, oddity, and penetrating power, they will perhaps frighten you because, in spite of your virtuous thoughts and actions, you have not assimilated a sufficient quantity of the substance of the Buddhas and Bodhisattvas.

Don't surrender to the fear that you are feeling.

Don't deviate from your path.

Contemplate the vision offered to you with serenity.

Calm your fears.

Don't surrender to desire.

Entrust yourself to He that enlightens,[5]

To the immortal Dordji semspa.

By the virtue of their essence the Liberation can come to you at this moment.

But your mental and material activity also manifests itself in thoughts of hate and jealousy and acts of ill will and wickedness that bring suffering to others. You have fed the desire for the bestial pleasures of lust and lasciviousness, you have devoted yourself to them and turned

---

4. These are three of the pâramitâ or excellent virtues.

5. *Vairocana;* in Tibetan *Nampar nang dzé (rnampar snang mdzad),* "who makes all appear"; a mystical personality of the Mahayanista pantheon.

away from Awareness, you have delighted in torpor and ignorance.

These are the forms taken by the angry deities and the guardians of the thresholds.

Their henchmen surround them like a tumultuous troop.

They have the forms of animals such as never existed in the world you have just left.

Surrounded by rays of multicolored light they raise themselves threateningly before you to bar your passage.

Strange sounds that produce fear will make themselves heard.

The clamor will grow.

Voices will bawl out: Hit! Hit! Kill! Kill!

Thus you will hear them and by the effect of your stupid actions be rendered deaf to the liberating truths that are being shouted to you.

Don't surrender to the fear that takes possession of you.

Resist the confusion that troubles your mind.

Nothing of what you see has any reality.

You are contemplating the contents of your mind filled with contradictory thoughts.

Deities with terrifying form will appear to you: Shindjé shépdo, Tandrin, Nampar gyalwa, Dutsikylwa.

And the angry faced Dakinis carrying goads, lassos, chains, and bells,[6]

Spinning all around you.

Don't fear them at all.

Don't try to flee.

These terrifying figures are the opposing aspect of the benign faces of the Buddhas and the Bodhisattvas that you previously contemplated.

They emanate from your own mind where the two aspects coexist.

---

6. They display themselves with half-human bodies and the faces of lions, wolves, and birds of prey with vulture beaks.

Within you are the five wisdoms,[7]
Within you are the five poisons.[8]
The dull and brilliant lights that appear to radiate toward you and penetrate your heart, in reality emanate from it.
What you see is only a reflection of the contents of your mind
Sent back to you by the mirror of the Void.
If this understanding that looms upon you provokes a terrible shock, you are feeling the fragmentation of the ethereal body[9] that you are still dragging behind you and you will be free of it.
However, the abilities you have at your disposal by virtue of this ethereal body
Can provide more substance to your illusion.
It is enough for you to think of a place to find yourself there immediately, even if it is at the other end of the world.
Don't use this power to wander in the places that you have frequented among those people for whom you still thirst because of past sensations.
If you are incapable of grasping the meaning of what has been taught and cannot make use of it to free yourself,
If the desire to exist in an individual form still possesses you,
You will be incapable of closing the mouth, which is like a gulf, yawning wide open, of the universal wheel where various wombs are ready to lure you.
You risk taking one of those paths lit by the dull light that seems restful and friendly on your eyes, which cannot sustain the burst of the radiant lights that have been shining on your path.

---

7. The five wisdoms: the wisdom of works, the wisdom that distinguishes and classifies, the wisdom that unifies, the wisdom that mirrors the game of cause and effect, and the wisdom of the sphere of the elements, which has awareness of the fundamental unity existing beneath apparent diversity.

8. The five poisons: covetousness, anger, lust, pride, and torpor.

9. The *djalus (hdjah lus)*, "the rainbow body": the illusionary body that is analogous to the "double" or "astral body" of occultists.

Your movements proceed from the illusion you preserve of the aggregation that has constituted your I and is now dispersing.

Among the multicolored rays of light encircling the saraband of howling and threatening deities who are in constant agitation all around you, there is a white ray, straight as a road stretching off into infinity.

It leads to the sphere of the gods, take it if you can. It is better to abstain, however, if you have rejected an individual existence on the wheel of existence.

Happy sojourns are unreal and transitory. Like bubbles on the surface of the ocean, they emerge from our mind in waves of sensation, then burst and are engulfed only to surge up again in new unstable formations, both agreeable and painful, following upon the heels of one another according to the incessant activity of various and contradictory energies.

If your propensities directed to the Good impel you irresistibly, you will follow this path of pale whiteness and for a time taste of the repose that awaits you where it leads.

If you have been fed on feelings of jealousy, violent ambition, and if your last thoughts forced you to enter the Bardo with your ethereal body imbued with combative influences, you will be tempted to take up the path of green light.

Resist your impulse, the green ray leads to the world of Lhah-ma-yin.[10] *They are perpetually at war with the Lha, vainly striving to scale the space that separates them from the world of faith and silence. They are ceaselessly vanquished and renew their efforts ceaselessly with infinite fatigue.*

---

10. The *Lha-ma-yin* (the non-gods) are the *Asuras* of Indian mythology, similar to the Titans. They are perpetually at war with the gods who forced them from their dwellings and took them for their own.

Turn aside if you can.

You could be drawn to the pale gold ray that buries itself beyond sight in the infinite distance. This is the path that leads to the world of men, to that world you have just left. There the individual will experience rare joy followed by much suffering, sickness, the loss of property, the loss of his closest friends and family, the infirmities of old age followed by the horrors of death which hurl them into the Bardo, the antechamber of new rebirths.

Recall all your memories of the vicissitudes of your numerous lives, reject the desire to feel anew the sensations of the dream in the human world.

Detach yourself.

Place yourself in the empty state of nonattraction and nonaversion. In the state of perfect mental immobility,

When your mental state resembles a lake whose water is without the least of undulations, like a perfectly polished mirror, then reality can find itself reflected there.

If your propensities are toward heaviness of mind and spirit, toward indifference, nourished by your actions, you will be drawn by a ray of blue-gray light.

Resist it, turn aside, if you can.

It leads to the unhappy world of animals who are incapable of attaining a Liberating Awareness.

Resist, resist, keep trying to resist it just one more time!

The dismal red ray attracts you, it leads to the frightful world of the Mi-ma-yin,[11] miserable beings whose figures are constantly tormented by

---

11. The *Mi-ma-yins* (the non-men) consist of numerous categories. Those described here are the *Yidag*, but others exist with nothing horrible about them such as genies, fairies, etc., some with a malevolent attitude toward mankind, the others more inclined to friendliness.

*needs that their lack of the appropriate organs does not allow them to
satisfy.*

*Evoke the memory of the Buddhas and their Doctrine, the compassionate
Bodhisattvas, your tutelary God,[12] and your wise Guru.*

*The beneficial influence of the thoughts associated with them can soften
the effect of your past bad deeds and block your entry onto the terrible
red path.*

*Not far from it there is an obscure path the color of smoke: it leads to the
regions of suffering, the hells where the duration of lives is long and
rare is the occasion of a death leading to a better life.[13]*

*Strongly evoke the memory of the Buddhas and the Bodhisattvas. Remind
yourself of the unreality of the visions that appear to you and take
domination over the movements of your mind. Form charitable thoughts
toward all beings.*

Don't abandon yourself to fear.

It is from you that the various ray-paths you have contemplated emanate.
It is in you alone that they exist as well as the worlds they lead to.

Chase away all feelings of attraction and aversion.

Remain indifferent and calm.

*If, because of the influence of the mental torpor to which you abandoned
yourself in the existence that you have just left, because of the evil
deeds that you have accomplished, compelled by your ignorance and
unhealthy propensities, you have remained bewildered and deaf to that
which has been taught to you, while advancing, without taking it into
account, among the phantasmagoria of the Bardo, try to hear it now.*

---

12. The *Yidan* of the Tibetans—the *Ishta dévata* of the Hindus.

13. The duration of a life in one of the hells can last for an extremely long time,
but there is always an end to it followed by a rebirth. No condition is eternal in
Buddhism.

The ethereal body that drags along behind you is imbued with your past desires and an avid thirst for sensations whose souvenirs haunt it and that the lack of flesh organs prevents it from satisfying. The desire for reincarnation is an intolerable torment for it.

This desire that you are holding without being aware of its nature is felt as an ardent thirst while you wander, harassed, across a desert of burning sand.

On your road you will spot a chörten[14] or several of them grouped together, or else you may see a covered bridge,[15] and you will desire to rest sheltered by them, but monstrous beings loom out of them. Some of these are animal headed, others are gigantic birds whose wings are studded with claws. They scream out strident cries and yells. They shake whips, a hurricane will seize you with its twisting winds, precipitating you forward as this troop of furious demons pursues you.

Along your route you can see temples and palaces constructed from gold and silver and adorned with precious stones. They are bathed in a sweet white light. Enter them if you can. The palaces and temples are symbolic wombs, and the threshold you cross takes you into the world of the gods where one emerges into life through a miraculous and pure birth[16] in the center of a blossoming Lotus bud.

If you are constrained to follow your route, compelled by the power of your past deeds, you will come across an agreeable, green grove. Ponderous fruits hang from the trees, and you will want to pick them to assuage your thirst.

Don't let yourself do so. What looks like a grove is actually the womb

---

14. A religious monument that is found everywhere, throughout Tibet.

15. Similar to the Chinese roof-covered bridges that exist in Tibet as well.

16. One emerges there miraculously, totally formed, without going through infancy, and one is born without the intervention of parents or the union of the sexes.

that causes rebirth into the disturbed world of the Lha-ma-yin[17] warriors.

You will also find yourself traversing expanses covered with dried and spiny thickets. Get yourself away from there, these are the wombs of miserable beings who are always greedy.[18]

You will see grottos and caverns, some of these are of an agreeable aspect offering restful shelter, the others are dark and dusty.

Don't allow yourself to venture into any of them. The first are the wombs of the animal world. Through them one is reborn as a horse, a dog, a buffalo, a wolf, a bear, a bird, a fish, or another bestial form. The others are the wombs through which one is reborn among the tormented beings of the infernal worlds from which one can only emerge after a long sojourn.

Prevent yourself from entering them.

You will see a lake or a river and on the banks are fertile, sunlit fields. You will want to seat yourself on the grass covered banks and assuage your thirst with the crystal-clear water sparkling before you. This charming landscape is the womb through which one is born into the land of human beings.

Be on the alert. Repress your desire.

Don't stop.

But the memory of the carnal sensations you abandoned yourself to in the course of your past life will goad the ethereal body that you are now dragging behind you.

Before you, all around you, humans are coupling with one another, animals are coupling with one another, you envy them and are drawn toward them.

If the effect of your propensities destines you to be reborn as a male, you

---

17. See previous note 10.

18. The *Yidag*, see previous note 11.

will feel a strong aversion for the males that you see. If your propensities destine you to be reborn female, you will feel a strong aversion for all the females you see.

Don't approach these couples you see, don't try to interpose yourself between them, to take the place of one of them, whether it is that of the male or the female, the human or the animal.

You will swoon from the sensation you are feeling and be conceived as a human being or as an individual of one or the other species of animals.

If you allow yourself to be detoured from your path here, you are now at the end of your sojourn in the Bardo.

You find yourself before Shindjé, the Lord of the Dead.

Your efforts to lie, to dissimulate the bad deeds that you have committed, will be in vain.[19] The forms of all your mental and physical actions will appear in the resplendent mirror held by the Supreme Judge.

However, listen to me a little longer.

Know that the figures, whatever form they take, that you can contemplate in the Bardo are unreal dream images that you have constructed and are projecting, without recognizing them as your own creations, and being frightened by them.

The mirror, in which Shindjé is appearing to read you, is your memory recalling the chain of events that are your past actions and they are judged according to the conceptions that you have formed.[20]

It is you alone who, by virtue of the dispositions within you, is going to pronounce sentence upon you and assign you to such and such a reincarnation.

No terrible God will compel you to go there.

---

19. An aspect that varies from what we are told in the Egyptian Book of the Dead where, through the knowledge of magical techniques, the deceased can fool the judge of the dead and hide from him the faults that they committed while living.

20. That is to say, according to your ideas and opinions concerning good and evil.

You will walk there of your own will.

The figures of the frightening beings that you see taking hold of you and pushing you toward your next rebirth are those which you yourself have made to assume the strength of the tendencies within you.

Know this, too,

Outside of your hallucinations, neither gods nor demons exist, nor does the Vanquisher of Death.[21]

Understand this and set yourself free.

An attentive reading of the Bardo Thödal can't fail to provoke in the reader countless reflections inspired by the diverse episodes of this singular voyage, which the author of the work has the disincarnated spirit of the deceased accomplish. Those, for example, who consider that the sum of the causes engendered by an individual's activity (karma)[22] ends with the death of that individual and that there is then nothing left to do but submit to the effects stemming from those causes, will be astonished to see disincarnate souls provided with the will that permits them to decide their future fate, without taking their karma into account. They will find astonishing as well that these opportunities of attainment—whether it be the "deliverance" from the wheel of reincarnations (*nirvana*) or whether it is fortunate reincarnations—will be found repeatedly in the course of the voyage through the Bardo.

---

21. Yamantâka; in Tibetan: *Djampal Shindjé gshév.*

22. Karma (action) is actually not quite the proper term to use in designating the "fate" assigned to an individual. Nevertheless, I employ it because it is probably familiar to most of my readers, who certainly understand that it is the individuals themselves who have manufactured the destiny that they must submit to by their works (karma). The Tibetans also make use of the Sanskrit term, *karma*, but more commonly they say *nieun ky lés* (past actions).

The initiates of the Bardo ritual declare that the repetitions found there are not useless and they give various explanations on this subject. I will try to present these arguments in a condensed form.

First of all, the warning that is given continually to the auditor of the text must always be kept present in the memory: the voyage described in the Bardo is not a real voyage, accomplished in real places. It translates, in images, the conceptions that have been registered in the intellect of the deceased. No new aliment is supplied to what already is there;[23] the mind simply "ruminates" on those conceptions of all kinds that it previously ingested.

I posed the following question to a lama who had contact with Christian missionaries on the Tibetan-Chinese border:

Will Christians who follow the religion of Issou (Jesus) enter the Bardo?

Certainly.

But they believe neither in the gods of the lamas, nor in reincarnation, nor in anything that is described in the Bardo Thödal.

They will enter the Bardo, but what they will see is Issou, the angels, the demons, paradise, and hell. In their mind they will go back to all the things that they have been taught and in which they believed. They will compel the resurgence before them of terrifying visions; judgment and the torments of hell. The images that populate the dream of their journey and its imaginary vicissitudes will be different from those experienced by a Tibetan, but it will be based on the same reality. The "memories"[24] that the individual

---

23. This opinion is subject to dispute. Certain people believe that the visions perceived and the sensations felt by the disincarnate soul in the Bardo furnish a new aliment to the weakened mental faculties that it still possesses and that this will in turn constitute the base for new causes, of varying efficacy, from which new effects will unfurl.

24. The *vâsanas* of Indian philosophy.

stockpiled during the course of his life will take shape and present themselves to him like a moving picture, and every disincarnate soul, whether Tibetan or Christian, will have a tendency to mistake for real events the episodes that supplant one another only in the mind.

The repetitions found in the text indicate that the memories and souvenirs in the mind of the deceased, the thoughts that still haunt him, give birth to various forms of hallucinations. In short, the traveler is an obsessive who turns a limited stock of impressions over and over again in his mind. Such is, at least, one of the explanations that was given to me.

As to the choice that the voyager seems free to make independently of the law of karma, we should make note of the numerous restrictions that accompany the reiterated exhortations of the guide who expresses himself through the intermediary of the text of the Bardo Thödal. Note the "turn aside, *if you can*" or, even better, the "*if your natural inclinations don't compel you,*" etc. We see by this that the disincarnated traveler is, just as we are, subject to the influence of the material and mental substances of which his momentary individuality is composed. Like us, he is governed by various habits that rule his behavior.

However, the teachings presented in the Bardo Thödal certainly appear to mark that this behavior is not subject to a rigid fatalism. Certain transpositions or combinations can come into play in the group of elements that comprise the traveler, thus giving the majority to those elements that will opt for a more favorable decision for the disincarnate soul. This decision will be made, as are our own, under the direction of the momentary composition of our personality. One is able to foretell probabilities in this regard, but never with absolute certainty.

Another point touched upon in the Bardo Thödal should still hold our attention. It is said to the dying person: "Each of the consciousnesses,[25] which, placed together, have formed your personality, by virtue of the physical organs whose material is decomposing, will pursue its own particular activity." Does the Bardo Thödal aim here to attribute a distinct perpetuity to each of the "consciousnesses"[26] that are going to separate? Does this mean that each of these "consciousnesses" will reincarnate in an individual whose physical organs will once more serve to support them? Is this the equivalent of regarding these consciousnesses as individual entities that, having inhabited the body of the deceased, are now temporarily homeless and consequently seeking, in one way or another, to continue their existence elsewhere? This concept cannot be sustained in Buddhism. No consciousness of form and color can exist without the contact of the eye with forms and colors. It is the same for all of the attached consciousnesses and for each of their respective sense organs. What we call "consciousness," learned lamas say, is a mental operation. It is certainly not a person.

However, the Tibetans retain the idea of multiple reincarnations of the same personality. We find it expressed, notably, by the three simultaneous reincarnations of the recognized division—spirit, word,

---

25. See previous notes.

26. "Consciousness" (in Tibetan *namparshéspa [rnampa shépa]*) signifies "awareness," that is, the act of taking into account the sensation felt by means of the contact that one or another of our senses provides for us. However, for the great majority of Tibetans, the abbreviated term *namshés* means almost exactly the same thing as is meant by the Indian *jíva*, an entity that transmigrates. It is this namshés that, in popular belief, travels in the Bardo; "it" is what our awarenesses are attached to; again "it," as we will see, is what drags an ethereal "double" through this voyage, the double that was joined with it during its terrestrial incarnation. The term *namshés* covers a multiplicity of meanings in Tibet, which are at times contradictory.

material form.[27] Thus, we understand that the "spirit" of a dead lama is represented by a certain *tulku*,[28] while two other lamas embody, respectively, his "word" and his "body." The two embodiments of word and body are rarely encountered, and in any case only the reincarnation of the "mind" or "spirit" truly counts. It is the only embodiment, practically speaking, that is considered the return of the deceased lama among the living and the only one to take possession of the chair, title, and property of his predecessor, that is to say, "takes back" possession of all that used to belong to him.

What becomes of these consciousnesses that separate? Nothing else befalls them, according to knowledgeable lamas, than what occurs at every instant; the energy of the various natures engendered by our mental activity becomes commingled with the flood of all the activities at work in the universe and overflows into the reservoir of consciousnesses—the *Alâya Vinâna* of Mahâyâna Buddhism—from which they emerge anew as so many "memories" and predispositions that incite new power currents and activities. Thus turns the "wheel," the samsâra.

However, we are told that some dying individuals will fight this dispersion of their consciousnesses and that, at times, they succeed in maintaining the unity of their personal grouping. They can even give one of them preeminence and project it into their next incarnation. This state is produced in the case of an individual who felt that by dying he was leaving a heartfelt task unfinished, or who simply desired to continue working on an accomplished task he feared would be abandoned with his departure from the world. Many other rea-

---

27. In Tibet, there is constant usage of these terms for designating the triple aspect of the personality: spirit, word, and physical form (*sems, ngag, lus*).

28. See note 29 for a definition of *tulku*. *Ed.*

sons are also presented as capable of provoking this desire to perpetuate a certain kind of activity in a new incarnation.

Numerous Tibetans believe that if the dying individual is endowed with mental powers and will of sufficient strength, he will succeed in achieving the reincarnation of the block of his personality, thus giving birth to a *tulku*. The variety of opinions that have been enunciated on this subject and the number of discussions they have given birth to are considerable.

We have just seen how the reincarnation of all the consciousnesses, or a notable portion of them, after the physical dissolution of the body in death creates the occasion for the existence of a tulku. It is rare that the individual who is considered a tulku has a clear awareness of his particular state of being. However, at times it appears that this awareness manifests in the proof of memories concerning facts from the previous life. Tibetans base the authenticity of the tulku on the "proofs" of this kind.

There exist hundreds of tulkus in Tibet, Mongolia, and other countries professing the faith of Lamaistic Buddhism; their respective importance varies according to the social or religious position occupied by the personality who started the line, at times very long, of these successive reincarnations. The three most eminent Tulkus[29] are the Dalai Lama, the Pentchen Lama, and the Lady Grand Lama Dordji Phagmo, abbess of the Samding monastery on the edge of Lake Yamdok, south of Lhasa.

Much has been written concerning the personality of the Dalai Lama, but in truth Westerners have no idea of what is actually in accordance with the orthodox doctrine of Tibetan Buddhism. Foreign writers commonly bestow such titles as "Living God,"

---

29. It should be recalled that *tulku (sprul s kus)* means "illusionary body," "body engendered by magic."

"Reincarnation of Buddha," "Spiritual Head of all Buddhists," and so forth on the Dalai Lama. A Dalai Lama is nothing of the sort. He is not a reincarnated god; and the Buddha, who has attained nirvana, doesn't reincarnate. No one among the Buddhists occupies a position similar to that of the pope in the Catholic Church. No one has the authority of dictating to Buddhists what they should or should not believe, which religious practices they should adopt, or if they should abstain from all ritual practice. Each Buddhist can adapt, according to his desire, the doctrines of whatever Buddhist sect seem best to him. A Buddhist from Ceylon feels no adoration for the Dalai Lama. He does think, however, that he professes a kind of degenerate Buddhism that has little in common with the original teaching of the historical Buddha, Siddhartha Gautama.

Just what is the Dalai Lama then, for the Tibetans, Mongolians, and others who share the beliefs of the Tibetans? First of all, he is the reincarnation of his immediate predecessor, and through him, a link in the chain of reincarnations that constitutes the lineage of the Dalai Lamas. (The current Dalai Lama, in 1960, is the fourteenth in the order of succession.)

It is an error to believe that the institution of the Dalai Lamas and their temporal powers dates back to Tsong Khapa,[30] the founder of the Gelegspa sect, which actually constitutes the church of the state. Neither Tsong Khapa nor his first successors at the head of the reformed clergy[31] bore this title. Neither did they exercise any temporal power. The title Dalai Lama (Dalai means "ocean" in Mongolian) was conferred by Altan Khan, a Mongol

---

30. Born in Amdo on the Chinese border around 1240.

31. Kas doup djé (Mkhas grub djé) and Gédun doub (Dge dun grub).

prince, to the third successor of Tsong Khapa, Sönam Gyatso.[32]

There was also a Mongol prince, Gushi Khan, who being instituted as the protector of the fifth Dalai Lama, vanquished the Prince of Tsang Province,[33] who had taken possession of Lhasa, and established this fifth Dalai Lama, Mga wong Gyatso, temporal sovereign of the provinces of U and Tsang.

Amdo and Khams, the regions neighboring China, were never subject to his power. Even though incorporated later into Tibet,[34] the control of the government seated in Lhasa has never been strictly established in these regions whose populations remain as ferociously independent as ever.

If the Tibetans regard the Dalai Lamas as incarnations of the same personality, this does not serve as the reason for the universal adoration they receive from Lamaism's faithful. This kind of serial reincarnation is the case for all the lama tulkus. This particular form of adoration is based on the belief in an intimate and mysterious union of the Dalai Lama with a mythical and symbolic personage of Mahâyâna Buddhism, the Bodhisattva Avalokiteshvara (in Tibetan, Chenrezigs).[35]

It was around 1650 that the fifth Dalai Lama, just installed in Lhasa as its temporal sovereign, deemed the time was right to heighten his already eminent situation by adding to it the prestige

32. Sönam Gyatso means "ocean of merits" or "virtues." The Mongolian term was therefore a translation of the name *gyatso*, which was that of this lama.

33. The Tsang pa, inhabitants of Tsang province (capital Jigatzé, seat of the Pentchen Lama, located to the west of U province with its capital Lhasa) have always aimed to maintain independence from the government of Lhasa.

34. Nominally.

35. It goes without saying that Chenrezigs is endowed, in popular belief, with a real existence and can be considered a deity.

of a mystical relative in the spirit world. He claimed to be inhabited by the spirit of Chenrezigs.

There was no question that this was not a reincarnation. The
Bodhisattva belonged to the spiritual plane,[36] and thus was neither
born nor died. It had no material body. It was the personification of
an abstract concept.

According to the ignorant majority of the Tibetan population,
Chenrezigs inhabits the Western Paradise of the Great Beatitude
(Noub Déwa chén), where he is always ready to give aid to his devotees
and to which he welcomes them at the end of their terrestrial existence. He is employed by the lamas officiating at the bedside of the
dying to project their minds into the realm of delights.

Returning to the Dalai Lama, the most correct way of understanding his position is to consider him an avatar, in the style of the
Indian avatars of the god Vishnu, such as Krishna and Rama among
others. The Dalai Lama is neither a god, nor is he an incarnation of
the historical Buddha; he is an avatar of Chenrezigs. At the same
time that he instituted himself as an avatar of Chenrezigs, the fifth
Dalai Lama declared his old master to be an avatar of Amithaba
(Odphagméd in Tibetan). This is the origin of the line of Pentchen
Lamas. It should be noted, in passing, that long before the creation
of the Dalai Lama, the greatest of the Tibetan Kings, Srong bstan
Gampo (641), was considered an avatar of Chenrezigs.

Touching on a matter closer to the theories concerning reincarnation by means of the tulkus is that of the "transference" (always
under the name namshés) of an individual into another individual.

---

36. These Bodhisattvas created by Mahâyâna Buddhism must be distinguished
from the human Bodhisattvas of primitive Buddhism. These latter were individuals who had attained a high degree of spiritual perfection and thus were reincarnated as perfectly enlightened Buddhas.

Death, a sojourn in the Bardo, and a rebirth play no role in this case.

This transference is called *powa*. We have already spoken of this adjunction to the ritual reading of the Bardo Thödal next to a dying individual and have even seen how sometimes this reading is omitted and replaced by the briefer process of the powa. The goal of this is to supplement the effort the disincarnate soul must make in the Bardo to ensure the success of his journey and lead it to a favorable conclusion.

The shouting of the syllable "hick!" in a particular tone of voice is said to provoke the namshés to gush out of the crown of the dying person's head, which causes it to be suddenly projected into the Paradise of the Great Beatitude.

The fashion in which "hick!" should be pronounced must be learned from a master properly initiated into the secrets of the powa ritual. A long apprenticeship is necessary to succeed in giving this exclamation the precise sound on which its effectiveness depends.

It is prohibited to follow "hick!," repeated three times at the dying person's bedside, with the exclamation "phat!" (pronounced "peth"). This expression is only emitted when it is certain that death is imminent and without remedy, for "phat!" following "hick!" inevitably causes death.

It is said that certain Tibetan yogis employ this procedure to commit suicide. In this way they project their consciousness (namshés) right to the Paradise of the Great Beatitude or another destination of their choice.

Finally, it should also be noted that the Hindus, like the Tibetans, attach a great importance to the exit of the spirit (namshés, jîva, soul) through the crown of the head. Its exit through any other point of the body is regarded as leading to an unpleasant reincarnation. It is probable that the Tibetans have borrowed this idea from India.

The shout of "phet" is also employed as an exorcism at the end of certain mantras and is regarded as having the power to destroy evil spirits. On the other hand, Milarepa attributes to this sound the power to bring about the reunion of elements, once these elements have been scattered, producing a conscious perception of objects. "Phet" therefore seems to be considered an agent to strengthen the unity of the personality when that unity is threatened with being broken apart.

Related to this theory concerning personality transference (powa) is another that seems to derive from the Chinese Taoist belief in the possibility of rendering oneself physically immortal. As we have just seen, in the powa it is a subtle part—immaterial or semimaterial—that is extracted from one individual and either grafted or introduced to another who has previously been emptied to receive it. The other kind of transference is totally different. It concerns the passage of an individual from the class of beings to which he belongs into another class of beings. It is not said that the person must die in order to achieve this passage, or that a subtle principle (mind, soul, etc.) must evacuate in another manner the physical force to which it was attached.

In order to understand this particularly Tibetan concept, it is necessary to recall their representation of the world. The Tibetans have borrowed from the Indians the theory concerning the three worlds—the world of desire (kâma loka), the material world dominated by instincts of attachment and covetousness; the world of pure form and abstract ideas (rupa loka) and the world without form (arupa loka), which is inconceivable to us.[37]

The world of desire, the one in which we exist, shelters six classes of beings: the gods; the non-gods (Titans, adversaries of the gods

---

37. In Tibetan, respectively, *Deu pai Khams (dod pai Khams)*, *Zugs kyi Khams (gzugs kyi khams)* and *Zugs méd kyi khams (gzugs med kyi khams)*.

whose dwellings they covet); the humans; the non-humans, which consist of a variety of beings, including genies and fairies of various categories, animals of all species, and the miserable beings whose constitution destines them for suffering.[38] Associated with the latter are the inhabitants of the various hells. None of these conditions of existence is eternal. Beings are born, endure their temporary sojourns, and die in their respective departments; then are reborn, either into the same class of beings they just left or into another class.

There is no insurmountable barrier between the different divisions of the worlds. Their inhabitants jostle each other continuously, generally without being aware of it, which is not to say these contacts are never inconsequential because they occur without their knowledge. Given the belief in this promiscuity, one can easily imagine the passage, under exceptional circumstances, of a being into another category—such as a human insinuating itself among the crowd of deities or genies after having acquired their physical and mental characteristics.

Even though the transmigration achieved by an individual during his lifetime is accepted in principle, it is generally unknown to the majority of Tibetans. Only certain masters have made an occasional reference to it within the hermetic circle of their disciples.

On the other hand, another kind of transformation is recounted in the biographies of several high lamas. It consists of the disappearance, the "volatilization," of the material body.

The case of Marpa and his wife, Dangmedma, is very well known, and it is very rare to encounter anybody who doubts that it is based

---

38. Such as the *prêtas*, whose bodies are gigantic and whose mouths are as narrow as the eye of a needle. This particular trait prevents them from absorbing the quantity of food that is necessary, and they suffer the torture of constant hunger.

on real events. The Tantric scholar Lama Marpa was seated in a meditation posture while holding Dangmedma in his arms, both of them totally absorbed in profound meditation. In the course of this, the physical material of their bodies was sublimated, leaving nothing behind but their empty vestments. The same phenomenon is recounted in regard to Reschungpa, a disciple of the ascetic poet Milarepa; Guesar de Ling, the chief warrior hero of the Tibetan national epic; and for several others as well.

The "transference" operates by various other means for other ends. These are guarded in strict secrecy and form part of the esoteric teaching that the masters of the occult sciences reserve for their most intimate disciples.

Certain transference procedures aim at assuring the perpetuity of the individual's conscious life—in other words that of his namshés—by transporting it outside of the body, which no longer serves as a convenient vehicle, to another corporal envelope that is more fit to the individual's personal plans. This is achieved without the intervention of death. The rupture caused by death and the subsequent reappearance of the namshés in another corporal envelope are thus avoided along with all the consequences that this entails—oblivion, forgetfulness, and so forth.

The namshés of the initiate installs itself directly in the body of an individual whose namshés it has dislodged or who it has reduced to a state of servitude through assuming mastery of the person housing it. This is a phenomenon analogous to possession. The body abandoned by the namshés either slowly declines or suddenly perishes.

This can be compared to situations in which a part of the mental and material union that constitutes the personality of an individual breaks apart before the actual moment of death. This person continues to accomplish his normal routine even though he is no longer "entirely" present in our world. Only those who possess clairvoyant talents and have been instructed in the occult conditions of life can perceive this particular state. However, the majority of Tibetans believe it to be true and accept with no astonishment the declaration made at times by lamas who have been called upon to preside at an individual's funeral: "This person has already been dead for two or three years or more." Psychic phenomena and sensations felt by certain people would appear to militate in favor of this bizarre theory.

The disaggregation of the spiritual components that, united with the material elements, constitute the living individual, doesn't occur in one fell swoop. All the Tibetan yogis, the *nalsjorpas,* declare that one can have "a foot in another world" and, moreover, that portions of our conscious personality can live simultaneously in different worlds, experiencing various kinds of existence. The Bardo Thödal, according to some, reflects the impressions felt by people in this situation.

Now let us return to the disincarnate traveler wending his way through the Bardo. We have seen that the namshés, which the reader of the Bardo Thödal is advising so lavishly, does not travel alone. It has a companion that it "drags[39] along behind and from which it tries to disengage as an obstacle to its own liberation." This companion is an ethereal body "imbued with the desires that the disincarnate soul has nourished during the life he has just left." It "has an ardent thirst for the sensations that it has known and which it can no longer feel for lack of the organs by whose intervention these sensations produced themselves."[40]

What is this companion of the namshés that has entered the Bardo with it? It is denoted as the *djalus (hdjah lus).*

---

39. See p. 51.
40. See p. 51.

The *djalus* is conceived as an entity that if not immortal can still continue to exist for a much longer time than the physical body. The term *djalus* is not in common use, save in literature, and the average Tibetan doesn't speculate on its nature. For the majority of Tibetans, the protean namshés fills all the various roles.[41] Literally, *djalus* signifies a body made of rainbows *(dja)*. This appellation is a poetic way of designating its subtle and illusionary character, similar to the rays of colored light that make up the rainbow.[42]

I am tempted to call this body a "double," similar to the Egyptian *ka*, a double that was, for the latter, distinct from the soul *(ba)*. This is the soul that the Tibetans seem to regard as immortal, whereas the double depends on the offerings made by its friends and family to survive. This is similar to the beliefs held by the Chinese Taoists.[43]

Even though the great majority of Tibetan people would never dream of discussing the nature of a double and the difference that exists between it and the namshés, nevertheless, this double plays an important role in their beliefs. It should be established from the outset that it is hardly granted any sympathy. If the namshés, while

41. In regard to *djalus* let's say that correctly and technically this term designates a lama who has successfully achieved an advanced degree of subtilization of his physical body, so much so that it dissolves. A phenomenon of this type previously alluded to is attributed to Marpa (tenth century), a learned translator of Sanskrit Buddhist texts and an adept of Tantric doctrines. When seated on his throne with his wife, Dangmedma, in the posture of sexual union (similar to the statues of Tantric deities), both became totally absorbed in their meditation and their bodies volatilized. Perhaps a comparison can be made here between this volatilization of the material body and the Taoist concept of the perfect individual who "climbs to Heaven in the middle of the day," that is to say, has attained immortality, leaving no physical remains in the tomb. See p. 63.

42. See p. 42.

43. See p. 107 for a comparable Hindu belief.

in the Bardo, is gently exhorted to separate from its former life, the relatives of the deceased urge it do so with such haste and by the use of such simplistic procedures that it would appear that this double is regarded as endowed with little intelligence.

A funereal repast is offered to the dead, during which the deceased is pressed to eat a large amount of food in order to have the necessary strength to accomplish the difficult journey that he or she is about to undergo. At the same time, the deceased is also urged to guard against any desires to return to his or her house or family members.

Accordingly, a relative or a village elder would make a speech to the deceased much like the following example:[44]

> Listen well, Tenzing,[45] you are dead. You have nothing left to do here. Follow your path.
>
> Your creditors have arrived,[46] they have seized your livestock and your horses. They have taken your children to serve as their servants; in this way they think to recoup some of what they are owed.
>
> Your wife is no longer in your home. She has been chased out of it so that your creditors can use your house or sell it.
>
> As she is still strong enough to work, Tseundup has taken her in. He will make her his second wife.
>
> If you view all of this, you will torture yourself over it. But you can prevent none of it, you can no longer plant a field or make use of tools. It is therefore useless for you to lurk around here. We have fed you well, that's enough. Go where you are supposed to go and don't come back here to trouble anyone.

---

44. This is something I heard myself.

45. The name of the deceased.

46. The orator can say this without question. There is no such thing as a Tibetan who is out of debt.

The spirit (the double) of the deceased is supposed to believe these lies and leave. On occasion, however, one insists on remaining, and then a lama must be called in, a *ngagspas* who knows the magic formulas; or if these don't work, a Bön can be called upon, who is even better because he is an adept of the pre-Buddhist religion of Tibet. The "ghost" that was not taken in by the ruse will be dealt with in a harsh manner. The power of special rituals will be directed against him, as they are against demons, and he will be chased away.

People of all nations are familiar with cases of haunted houses and souls in distress lurking around their family members. There is nothing particularly different about these incidents in Tibet except for the exhortations of the deceased's friends and family enjoining him or her to get away from them.[47]

More interesting is what we are told concerning the manifestations of doubles of living individuals. Tibetans mention several kinds of these:

Those which have been achieved voluntarily.

Those which have been achieved involuntarily.

Those in the course of which the body of the individual, whose double has become partially disassociated, remains inert—either naturally asleep or in a cataleptic state.

Those during which the body behaves naturally while the double that has become separated from it makes a show of activity at a place some distance away.

The double is not immaterial, but its constituent matter is very tenuous. As a general rule, the double remains invisible. When it

---

47. This can be compared to the Chinese who, conversely, strive to retain the souls of those they have loved.

becomes visible, its form habitually appears as a carbon copy of the material body.

Certain people affirm that human beings are not alone in possessing a double. According to them, animals, plants, and all the bodies that we perceive under a solid aspect have a subtle form associated with them. Various opinions are expressed on the subject of the double; among others are those that represent it as a natural emanation that all bodies release and also as an extention of their natural range.

Even though generally inactive—or giving the appearance of being so—the double seems to possess its own kind of individuality that allows it to succeed at times in freeing itself from dependency on the body. Ordinarily it is only during periods of sleep, whether natural or artificially induced, that it can escape the control that we normally exercise over it. Consciously or not, the human being keeps his double prisoner. Perhaps the double carries within itself an obscure instinct that inclines it to seek its liberation. Questions of this kind are disputed among the occultists of Tibet, but the majority of their compatriots limit themselves to noting the curious phenomena that come to their attention without troubling themselves about discovering their mechanics.

The double, liberated and made visible, appears to have the ability to behave like a normal person. It can thus present an illusion to those who perceive it, but most frequently it wanders invisibly without its presence arousing suspicion, witnessing scenes that certain individuals will recount upon awakening.

I have heard a peasant recount how—while he was seen sleeping in his house—he had been at the home of a person well known to his audience who lived at some distance from the village in which this peasant lived. He had witnessed this man selling a horse and the haggling for which this sale provided an occasion. When the information was examined, it was found that all the details of this

event proved to be exact. One fact in particular stood out: the nego-
tiations concerning the horse were pursued to an abnormally late
hour because the buyer desired to have the sale concluded without
waiting until the next day because he wished to have the beast early
in the morning. At this time the peasant claiming to have been present
at the home of the horse's seller was already asleep. Analogous accounts are heard frequently, and the Tibetans accept them without
any great show of emotion.

Now we will view their amplification in regard to the *deslogs*. The
term *deslogs* literally means: "returned from the beyond." It doesn't
signify "ghosts" as it would in the West because the deslogs are not
dead. Rather, this term refers to men or women who have remained
in a state of lethargy for abnormally long periods of time, several
days or even longer.

Accounts mention contemplative hermits (*gomchens*) who have remained completely insensible to the world around them for periods
of several months at a time, in the state of *samâdhi*.[48] But their case is
very different from that of the deslogs. Equally different are the
Indian yogis who, after a specific kind of training, have themselves
buried alive. They are then drawn back from their tombs, alive, after
a period that has been said to have lasted for as long as several
months.

These facts, whatever your opinion may be of them, have no
bearing whatsoever on the deslogs. There is no training or prepara-
tion involved with them at all. This phenomenon occurs in a completely unexpected and involuntary fashion. A sleeping man or

---

48. *Samâdhi* is a state of perfect mental concentration during which physical sensation is completely abolished and the rate of breathing has become singularly
slowed. It is the end result of various degrees of contemplative meditation in
almost all the mystical sects.

woman suddenly becomes unconscious and presents the appearance of a corpse. There is no difference at all except that their bodies don't rot, and the experience ends with their reawakening.

In sum, the case of the deslogs is analogous to that of those individuals who, during their sleep, seem to divide in half and wander about with just a portion of their personality. Only the abnormal duration of their cataleptic state differentiates the deslogs from these individuals. However, it can be noted that whereas the tales recounted by the ordinary sleepers generally concern terrestrial sites and human individuals, the deslogs depict fantastic personages and regions that give those hearing them reason to believe that they have truly breached the borders of the world adjoining our own. Often the pilgrimages that the deslogs claim to have achieved resemble those of the disincarnate namshés in the Bardo, such as they are presented in the Bardo Thödal.

Other descriptions and adventures sometimes reflect popular belief concerning the various paradises and the hells. Demons play a great role therein.

One has, therefore, every reason to believe that while the body remains inanimate, the mind of the deslog continues its normal activity and, just as in dreams, manufactures images with the elements that have been gathered together and stockpiled in the course of his or her active, normal life. It would be rash, however, to claim the capability of meaningfully explaining the origin and nature of the thoughts and visions that present themselves to the mind in the time that elapses between the moment where the dying individual appears to have broken all ties with this world and the moment when he will definitively sink into unconsciousness and oblivion.

Do unconsciousness and oblivion truly exist? What was in existence yesterday exists today and will exist tomorrow, and will, under different forms, exist forever, guarding its effectiveness. Perhaps the deslog has half opened a door to a warehouse of memories. Perhaps he is only, as perhaps all of us are, nothing but living memories. What has been cannot cease to be.

The tales of the deslogs don't always concern themselves with fantastic voyages. During my stay in Lhasa there was talk of a deslog. It concerned a man known to have never left his own village. None of his close relations, nor the people he frequented, had ever traveled. They were all illiterate. This man, awakening after several days of lethargy, recounted how he had gone to Mongolia and was present at a learned discussion between lamas. The man described the locations where he found himself and repeated entire phrases of the conversations he had witnessed, of which he understood nothing. The subjects under discussion were totally alien to him and considerably exceeded his comprehension. He had grasped nothing but the sound of the words; he didn't even doubt that the Mongolian lamas were using a literary Tibetan language that plays, for the adepts of this discipline, the same role Latin once did for Europeans.

I haven't seen this man personally, but serious individuals worthy of respect accepted the authenticity of this account. Inquiries revealed that the discussion recorded by the man did indeed take place during an assemblage of lamas.

In cases of this type, there is often such a presence of veracity in the description of the places the sleeper says he has visited and the events he affirms to have witnessed that one has some trouble at maintaining their incredulity intact. Obviously, it can always be asked—and it is wise to do so—if either the person dreaming or any of those with whom he has been in contact has known the facts recorded, even though they may not remember. Telepathy may play a role here similar to that it appears to play in other situations.

Even though the involuntary wanderings of the double generally occur during the sleep of the individual to which the double is normally attached, it is not, however, always so. The apparition of people in places far from those where they are to be found devoting themselves to their normal occupations doesn't seem to be very rare in Tibet. I have witnessed several cases like this and have mentioned those that appeared the most characteristic in a previous book.[49] I will give myself the permission to reproduce here the relevant passage:

A young man in my service had gone to visit his family. I had granted him three weeks' leave, after which he was to purchase a food supply, engage porters to carry the loads across the hills, and come back with the caravan.

Most likely the fellow had a good time with his people. Two months elapsed and still he did not return. I thought he had definitely left me.

Then I saw him one night in a dream. He arrived at my place clad in a somewhat unusual fashion, wearing a sun hat of foreign shape. He had never sown such a hat.

The next morning, one of my servants came to me in haste. "Wangdu has come back," he told me. "I have just seen him down the hill."

The coincidence was strange. I went out of my room to look at the traveler.

The place where I stood dominated a valley. I distinctly saw Wangdu. He was dressed exactly as I had seen him in my dream. He was alone and walking slowly up the path that wound up the hill slope.

I remarked that he had no luggage with him and the servant who was next to me answered, "Wangdu has walked ahead, the load-carriers must be following."

49. Alexandra David-Neel, *Magic and Mystery in Tibet* (1932; reprint, New York: Dover, 1971), 308.

Two other men also witnessed Wangdu climbing the mountain.[50]

We both continued to observe the man. He reached a small *chörten*, walked behind it, and did not reappear.

The base of this chörten was a cube built in stone, less than three feet high, and from its needle-shaped top to the ground, the monument was no more than seven feet high. There was no cavity in it. Moreover, the chörten was completely isolated: there were neither houses, nor trees, nor undulations, nor anything that could provide a hiding in the vicinity.

My servant and I believed that Wangdu was resting for a while under the shade of the chörten. But as time went by without his reappearing, I inspected the ground around the monument with my field-glasses, but discovered nobody.

Very much puzzled, I sent two of my servants to search for the boy. I followed their movements with the glasses but no trace was to be found of Wangdu nor of anybody else.

The same day a little before dusk the young man appeared in the valley with his caravan. He wore the very same dress and foreign sun hat which I had seen in my dream and in the morning vision.

Without giving him or the load-carriers time to speak with my servants and hear about the phenomenon, I immediately questioned them. From their answers I learned that all of them had spent the previous night in a place too far distant from my dwelling for anyone to reach the latter in the morning. It was also clearly stated that Wangdu had continually walked with the party.

During the following weeks I was able to verify the accuracy of the men's declarations by inquiring about the time of the

---

50. This statement is not included in the Dover edition. *Trans.*

caravan's departure at the few last stages where the porters were changed. It was proved that they had all spoken the truth and had left the last stage with Wangdu, as they said.

Many people attribute phenomena of this genre to the movements of the double, but others are inclined to see in them, as in the previously mentioned case, the effect of telepathic transmission, even if it is achieved unintentionally. Sometimes, they explain, an individual who is apt to receive the transmission visualizes the exact image that is mentally projected toward him; sometimes he deforms it with the unconscious addition of details of his own creation by blending it with the ideas and "memories" that are to be found inscribed at that time, in his mind.

It is extremely rare that these apparitions occur as audible phenomena. As a general rule the double remains mute.

In the same way that the existence and the nature of the double have given rise to numerous controversies, another question concerning them has, in equal measure, attracted the attention of certain Tibetan thinkers. Can the double, obedient to impulses coming from the individual to which it is bound, commit good or evil physical actions manifesting tangible results? The ignorant majority of Tibetans have no doubt that an initiated magician can kill with the strength of his thought and conserves a power of this type, even after death. However, the learned Tibetan adepts of the occult sciences have not rushed to any conclusions on this subject or others like it.

Can the double devote itself to an efficient activity in its travels? Can it perform a task as the instrument of the will of another? Is it capable of developing a will of its own?

Opinions are split on these questions. Outside of the purely academic discussions these questions inspire, people remain convinced that the acts they commit while dreaming, whether it is a deslog dream or one that occurs in the course of their usual night's sleep, have material effects. Some of these effects are apparent, others remain hidden.

A merchant from the land of Kham was thus convinced that he had murdered his brother. The motive of his action was simple. This man was the younger brother in a peasant family, and he desired to quit the farmer's life for that of commerce and become wealthy; this is a dream of almost all Tibetans.

The young man called Tharchin had the occasion of performing several services for a rich merchant inhabiting the area of Dangar and had spent several months staying in his house. The time came when the merchants formed a caravan to journey to Lhasa, and he desired to be hired by his employer as an aide accompanying the shipment of his goods. He viewed this as the first step in the desirable career of a trader.

So, what happened? His brother was chosen to accompany the merchant and, furthermore, to assist in the transactions at Lhasa as a head clerk. The merchant appeared to be full of affection for his new employee and the frustrated younger brother foresaw the possible result of that infatuation.

The merchant had no son of his own, only a daughter of marrying age with an attractive face. Custom required that her father, desirous that after his death his daughter enjoy the goods that he had amassed, give her a husband of his choice, a man known by him as being a capable successor to manage his affairs and one whom he would make his heir. If the younger brother was fully confident in his own intelligence, he in no way underestimated his elder brother's capabilities, and he understood that his brother could be chosen later as son and heir, just as he had been for head clerk.

Then what? What of him? He would have to return to his miserable farm and toil on its three or four small fields until the end of his life. . . . Never would he accept that. A ferocious wave of hatred

rose up in him against this brother, whom he foresaw taking possession of the fortune that he had hoped to possess himself one day.

The day of departure arrived. The mules, loaded down with their
cargo of merchandise, were drawn away by several servants. The
merchant and his head clerk followed, mounted on the better animals. Cries wishing them a fortunate journey followed them out.
They responded to these merrily, and the eyes of those remaining
behind followed them until they were lost from view. The younger
brother was one of their number.

The same evening he left and, with no settled plan in mind, me-
chanically returned to the paternal home. During the several days it
took to attain his goal, he didn't stop once constantly brooding over
his deception all the while. He arrived worn out and battling a high
fever and let himself fall onto the thin cushions that served as both
chair and bed.

The next day he was almost unconscious and painfully swallowed
the sip of tea his sister offered him. His parents tried in vain to get
him to eat. He regarded them with a fixed stare, seeming not to see
them. This state lasted for three days; then that evening, he died.

Two lamas were called upon to recite the customary texts during
the time preceding the funeral. The surrounding countryside was
not wooded, thus there was no question of cremating the body. It
was customary to take the body to a remote spot in the mountains
and leave it there for the *rogyapas*[51] to tear to pieces, out of fear that
a demon would inhabit it otherwise. The dismembered remains would
be left to the vultures.

The rogyapas would return after several days, gather up the bones
now cleaned by the raptors, and grind them up. The resulting powder

---

51. Those who dismember the corpse to prevent its reanimation by demons.
Trans.

would be blended with clay and used in the manufacture of a tsa tsa,[52] which the family of the deceased would then have erected in a purified location.

Rather than try to recount the following drama myself, I prefer to reproduce the fantastic and somewhat incoherent tale as it was told to me, some years later, by the person who had played its main role:

> I was drunk, that is certain. I could feel it. I had gotten drunk with my friends more than once; I knew what to expect. But on this day I don't recall either having drunk anything or of being among a company of revelers. However, I was drunk. It seems to me that I was being swung back and forth . . . as if I was being weighed. It didn't end there. I felt a slight shock and the swaying motions ceased. Then I don't know what happened.
>
> Next I remember thinking about my brother . . . I saw him proudly disappearing into the distance with the merchant by his side. They continued on their way to Lhasa.
>
> Where could the caravan have arrived at by now? I forced myself to count the number of days that had passed since its departure; I don't know how, but I knew I would rejoin it further along the trail.
>
> Was I lying down, seated? I can remember nothing of it, did I stand up? I don't remember now, but suddenly I found myself on the trail to Lhasa, and I was advancing along it quite quickly. Was I walking along it? I don't recall.
>
> I rejoined the caravan. It had entered a much narrower area, and the mules were skirting the edge of a rocky terrain that

---

52. A kind of minature chörten made from a blend of clay and the ground bone of the deceased that serves as a funeral monument. *Trans.*

stretched far below them. They were advancing in single file. I saw my brother remaining a little bit behind. He was wearing the beautiful *pourouc* robe that his boss had given him.

Ah! Wouldn't he cut a fine figure among the merchants he was going to meet in Lhasa. And henceforth he would be *Kushong tshongpa* and later *Kushong tshongpa pân*,[53] to be received with respect at all the good inns. That is what I could have been—and I was going to be nothing more than a dirty peasant. He had stolen my chance; he had stolen the happiness from my life . . . the back of his large pourouc robe fascinated me.

How was it that I found myself right behind him? How did I happen to have the long iron tipped pilgrim staff? I don't know. I raised the staff with its iron tip aloft, and I struck my brother twice in the back with all my strength. He fell from his horse and rolled all the way down from the top of the path to the valley bottom far below.

I saw several servants running . . . and then saw that they were carrying my brother. Our employer was there. My brother had been laid on the ground and he wasn't moving. I understood he was dead. I had killed him. I am not too sure; I believe that I was happy and that I also felt fear.

I don't know how I found myself, all at once, close to the convoy of merchandise that had been on its journey for more than a month and should have been far away. And I don't know how I had removed myself from the spot where my brother had fallen from his mule when I hit him.

It was barely dawn, I could see the sky above me, I could feel that I was lying down. I could tell that I was stretched out along the ground. I had been placed in a hollow spot on the ground.

---

53. My lord the merchant; my lord the chief merchant.

Higher up there were several vultures perched around me and still. They were watching me. I moved my arm, they took flight.

I believe that all of this must have occurred over a long period of time. But I believe that I think that now because I have had time to reflect on it. I was not thinking at the time when I was coming back to awareness. When I began thinking, I told myself that I was dead and in the Bardo. But I saw nothing that is described in the book of the Bardo, neither the Bodhisattvas nor the terrible gods similar to those that are painted on the temple walls. I had seen nothing of the kind. I was not dead.

And all at once, I remembered: I had struck my brother with my staff, he had fallen . . . I had murdered him. I didn't regret it but I was scared. I had committed a crime.

I then saw that I was naked. That was strange. And why was I stretched out on the ground here instead of at the farm? I remembered going to sleep there, and I also remembered having seen the departure of the merchandise convoy of the merchant who was my employer.

When Tharchin recounted this tale many years after these events, his memory was still resistant concerning what could have occurred between the time he recalled returning to the farm after the departure of his brother with the merchant and the time when he regained consciousness, naked, in a hollow in the mountains, surrounded by vultures.

But the subsequent events he could remember quite clearly. He had returned to the farm. He had been welcomed with cries of terror. "Ro lang! Ro lang!"[54] screamed the people, and they threw

---

54. The Tibetans believe that, at times, demons enter the cadavers of the dead and then raise them back up from which derives the name: *ro* cadaver *lang* which rises

stones at him as well as flaming brands pulled from the fireplaces. In vain he tried to explain, to protest that he was not dead, that he had only had the appearance of being so, that he was a deslog.

No one would listen to him. The people talking among themselves only repeated that his cadaver had been consigned to the rogyapas to be cut into pieces, that they should have done so and next, that they should have ground up the bones pecked clean by the vultures to make the tsa tsa.

Several days had passed. The rogyapas hadn't returned yet. Why? No one had any idea. What was certain was that a demon had entered into the intact corpse and reanimated it. The people shouted to one another, but all were rendered mad by the terror inspired by the sight of the one they took for a demon, and they continued to scream exorcisms and hurl stones at him.

Tharchin fled.

Next? Next, he had run straight before him and encountered an encampment. He was fearful of any further misapprehensions on his behalf and presented himself as a wretched horseman traveling alone, who had been attacked by brigands and completely stripped of all he owned. They had taken his horse and even all his clothes.

There was nothing exceptional about such a misadventure. The travelers were put totally at ease and took pity on him. They provided him with some provisions, an old robe, and some boots and let him continue on his way toward the place he had believed it best to tell them he was heading.

The rest was the banal story of a poor devil whose courage and

---

up. These demons then run about the countryside and are extremely wicked. It is to avoid this possession of the corpse that the dead who are not cremated are often cut up into pieces. However, others, especially monks, are also thrown into rivers that are all alleged to pour their waters into the Ganges.

good fortune led him to rebuild a normal life for himself. He had become the servant of a merchant, and then had some dealings on his own account.

What was interesting about the story he recounted was his firm conviction that he was his brother's murderer. He had been able to inform himself about his brother later on. The latter had indeed died as in his vision. He had suddenly fallen from his mule and rolled over a cliff, his head hitting the rocks. He was dead on the spot.

The story of this deslog was suitable to feed conversations concerning the often discussed subject of the possibility possessed by the double to commit actions that have a material result. Those that accept this possibility find confirmation of their beliefs in the story of Tharchin the deslog. The others still maintain that it results from the intervention of telepathy.

Yes, they say, the fatal accident took place. Tharchin, whose hateful thoughts were completely concentrated on his brother and who wished for his death, remained in telepathic communication with him. Who knows if his thoughts didn't have an effect on the behavior of his brother, troubling him and provoking the clumsiness that led to his fall? At the very least he was able to feel and visualize what was occurring and by rejoicing in it attributed the blame for it to himself.

As for me, my reflections took me in another direction. I wondered why Tharchin had not been dismembered by the rogyapas. They had carried him; this appeared to explain the swaying motion that Tharchin had perceived, even though he was unconscious to all appearance. And then the rogyapas had undressed him and taken his belongings, which are theirs according to custom. Something must have prevented them from accomplishing their duty. But who? How? In Tibet, nobody feels very comfortable in the presence of a corpse—even the professional rogyapas—because demons are lurking around it. An incident that appeared to signal a demoniacal intervention could have occurred and they could have fled.

These were only my suppositions. They were plausible. I wasn't in a position to conduct any investigations concerning an event of almost thirty years ago and one that only interested me because of the attitude of the man who believed that he had killed by his phantom intermediary.

The questions of continuance and reincarnation are presented differently according to whether they concern a double or a tulpa.[55] First of all, it should be noted that when the term *reincarnation* is employed it is understood in the literal sense as a "return into the flesh." The spiritual part of a deceased person (what we know as its ego), deprived by death of the material envelope that sheltered it, reclads itself in a new envelope.

The Tibetans don't speak of a "return into the flesh," they simply say "previous life," "future life." Therefore, they have complete latitude to conceive, no matter under what form, these two lives between which is placed the one that is presently theirs. The great majority of Tibetans don't fail to represent their past and future lives to themselves as elapsed or elapsing anew as a member of one or the other six classes of beings who populate the universe;[56] they believe they have had and will have again an autonomous personality (a namshés) reclad in a material envelope.

It is not always the same with the intellectuals. They envision rebirths of an immaterial order: rebirth in the world of ideas; the perpetuity of ideas already proclaimed, communicated in one way or another to another person, or simply secretly conceived.

---

55. Magical or illusionary body. See p. 86.
56. The six classes of beings. See p. 61.

Although not manifested overtly, these ideas do not remain inactive. Each of our mind's movements[57] projects into the universe currents of force that can implant tendencies in receptive individuals that incline them to understand, and act in a manner more or less in conformity with, the transmitters of these forces. These transmitters can be both deceased and currently living people.

In the small circles where such things are discussed, some take this even further and advance the possibility—truly even the probability—of the reincarnation of thoughts, achieved by the birth of individuals directly animated by certain types of thoughts, coming from either deceased or living individuals. This is somewhat close to what Tibetans say occurs in the case of the lama tulkus, those whom foreigners improperly designate as "living Buddhas," the Dalai Lama being the most notable example of this kind of reincarnation. Regarding this series of tulkus, it is believed that the namshés, in this case the spirit of an eminent individual, has begun the series of reincarnations by reappearing in this world after death by means of a child whose physical form it has occupied since the time of its conception.

In contrast, death doesn't play a necessary role in the reincarnation of ideas. The idea emanating from a living individual has no need of that person's disappearance in order to proceed onward and take up residence in a newborn. It can even solicit individuals of different sexes and cause their union in view of procreating a being that it will imbue, a being that will represent and manifest it on the physical plane. In fact, this theory attributes an actual personality to the idea. It presents the idea as the equivalent of a real individual, endowed with will and awareness[58] that it inherits from those who conceived

---

57. The *samskaras* mentioned in Buddhism; the *vritti* that Patanjâli, the founder of Yoga, urged his followers to master.

58. The namshés depicted in the Bardo Thödal possesses these qualities.

and projected it by the strength of their desire for eternal life.

Our obsessive desire for permanence displays limitless ingenuity. Countless concepts have been engendered seeking assurance for the continued duration of a personal *I*, no matter how essentially transitory this *I* is.

The succession of causes and effects involved in reincarnations or physical or mental rebirths leads us back to a question that we have already noted: is the double or the *tulpa* capable of achieving a physical action followed by tangible results? We have seen that some are persuaded that this is indeed so, basing their opinion on precise facts that appear to support and justify this belief.

What is a tulpa? A tulpa is a magical creature. The eminent adept of the occult sciences is believed capable, through the strength of his mental concentration, of projecting tulpas in the forms of humans or animals that he utilizes according to his needs, often to execute acts that he himself can only wish for or imagine.

In legends and traditions we see the tulpas behaving like ordinary individuals. They are regarded as being capable of killing a man, working a field, marrying a woman, etc. We also see other tulpas accomplishing extraordinary acts that spring from magic. Nothing can stop them. They can instantaneously cross mountains by rising in the air above them, they can pass through walls, appear and disappear without leaving a trace, and so on.

Tulpas figure in the biographies of lamas, contemplative hermits, and heroes such as Guésar de Ling,[59] as well as historical personalities such as one of Tibet's most glorious kings, Srong bstan Gampo.

---

59. His story furnishes the subject of Tibet's national epic—its *Iliad*. Guésar de Ling, around whom so many legends have accumulated, really existed around the seventh century A.D. One can refer to my book, *La Vie surhumaine de Guésar de Ling*.

I will quote a passage from his biography here.

> Srong bstan Gampo thought that in order to assure the pros-
> perity of Tibet it would be good to bring the statue of a god that
> would protect it there. He had been miraculously informed that
> such a statue existed in Ceylon on the edge of the sea. This statue
> represented Chenrezigs.[60] No human hand had been its creator,
> it had emerged on its own.[61] It was buried under a sandalmaker's,
> behind a statue of Vishnu, at a spot where elephants were in the
> habit of sleeping.
>
> This sign was rather vague. The king was aware that he couldn't
> undertake a long voyage and conduct a prolonged search him-
> self. A tulpa would be more apt than he or any other man to
> triumph over the obstacles that such an enterprise would entail.
>
> Engendered by the strength of the king's thought, a person-
> age sprang out from between his eyebrows, at the spot where
> they meet on the bridge of the nose. This magic individual had
> the look of a Buddhist monk.[62] He was named Akaramatishila,
> and under this name he led a very long and active career that has
> been narrated for us by Tibetan historians.[63]
>
> Needless to say, Akaramatishila succeeded in discovering the

---

60. His original name in Sanskrit is Avalokiteshwara.

61. The number of objects that are reputed to be autogenous in Tibet is
considerable.

62. Thirteen centuries later, I succeeded, by a prolonged exercise of mental concentration inspired by the procedures of Tibetan Yoga, to produce the illusion of
an analogous person that was seen by one of my visitors. See *Magic and Mystery in
Tibet*.

63. See the summary of his adventures in my translation of Tibetan texts, *Textes
tibétains inédits*.

statue and brought it to Srong bstan Gampo. He performed still more missions, then his role finished; the king drew the tulpa's sustaining energy back into his mind. The tulpa broke apart and diluted itself into a ray of light that buried itself between the king's eyebrows and returned to the mental source from which it had been engendered.

The example offered by the tulpa of Srong bstan Gampo (there are hundreds of other analogous examples) fully informs us about the opinion of the Tibetans on the tulpa's capability to act as a real person and obtain the same kind of physical results.

Let's stop for a minute at the term *real*, which I have employed for lack of one that is more suitable. According to Tibetan scholars, there are various forms and degrees of reality. A tulpa, the creation of thought, possesses its own kind of reality. It is inferred that the effects of its activity have a degree of reality equivalent to that of its owner or a degree approaching that of the people and objects that we see in dreams.

These determine the sensations in us that are analogous to those we would feel if the scenes viewed during the dream had been experienced in a waking state. These sensations sometimes persist after awakening, and Tibetans never fail to cite the case of the man who dreamed he was caned and on the next day felt stiff and bruised.[64]

The acts accomplished by a tulpa are often presented as having very durable effects that are equal to those performed by a normal individual. No matter the degree of reality accorded to the tulpa, it

---

64. Objections can be made that it was because he felt stiff and bruised that he dreamed he was caned, but the Tibetans present other examples such as burn marks left on the body that one has inflicted or seen inflicted on themselves in dreams, as well as other cases.

arises that this entity, created and sustained by thought, must disappear when it ceases to be animated by that thought. We have seen how the tulpa Akaramatishila dissolved when his creator, King Srong bstan Gampo, no longer had need of his services. Is it always thus?

It has been stated earlier that the double and—even more so—the tulpa gradually tend to acquire a personality distinct from that of the individual on which it is dependent and that these doubles can sometimes prosper on their own, at least partially. Then, I am told, the same thirst for perpetual life that lives in us awakens in the rudimentary consciousness that can come to life in the tulpa. This gives rise to fantastic struggles between the entity and its creator, who strives to bring it back and reintegrate it.

That such struggles may take place in the domain of the imagination is very probable. Although to my knowledge no convincing examples exist of a double killing the material body to which it was joined, there are in Tibet an abundance of tales of tulpas that murder their creators.

Similar stories concerning robots destroying those who have built them are common currency in all the countries of the world, but those in Tibet are particularly frightening, especially those depicting combat that takes place on the mental plane. It is precisely because the material element is excluded that their truthful character holds our attention.

Even though we are taking into account that our thoughts are moving into the realm of the phantasmagorical, perhaps by extricating the facts from the "embellishments" with which the popular imagination has covered these incidents, we will discover material here that may be of interest to mental research.

In illustration of this I would like to present an opinion I heard expressed by a *gueshes*[65] in Khams. "We mustn't, " said this scholar,

---

65. A *gueshes* is a graduate in literature and philosophy from a monastical university.

always present the tulpas as fantastic beings. Yes, certain individual entities among them have been truly capable of being created all of a piece by the strength of thought and have accomplished extraordinary deeds, but there are many others in existence. These are indistinguishable from the individuals we rub elbows with on a daily basis. However, most of the time, it is beyond a shadow of a doubt, they are robots animated by foreign influences. The Tibetans depict them as having been emptied of their own minds and their physical form occupied by a namshés that has lost its owner in the course of a transference ritual (powa).

The description given by this gueshes applies to the phenomenon of mind transmission. The individual who is more or less partially transformed into a tulpa has assimilated the alien mind while hearing a speech, reading a book, or during a conversation. Very often this implantation has been made without his awareness, and subsequently, the borrowed ideas and convictions thus installed within control his behavior, even though he considers himself "entirely free and acting of his own free will."

The world is full of tulpas of this kind. Shouldn't it be said that the world contains nothing but tulpas? None of us is autogenous. We are physically and mentally issued from anterior causes, we incarnate tendencies and alien thoughts; this is the precise definition of a tulpa.

Here again we touch upon the problem of perpetual life and immortality and it should be repeated: none of the elements that form the group I call *I*, today will perish. They existed for a long time before being gathered together to constitute this current and transitory *I*. Tibetan masters train their disciples *to see* this tableau of their perpetual life.

Having seen that the Tibetans accept the possibility that the tulpa and perhaps the double as well can commit deeds that produce tangible results on the material plane, the question of responsibility follows. Who is responsible for an act committed by a double or a tulpa?

The word "responsibility" cries out for explication. As always, one must distinguish between the beliefs held on this subject by the average Tibetan and Indian and by the intellectuals of their respective countries. Among the former, the idea of responsibility evokes thoughts of punishment and reward. With the latter, the author of a material or mental action (thought, etc.) will only be subjected to the effects of the cause that he has put into motion with that physical deed or thought, which itself is the result of multiple anterior causes.

The average Tibetan would never cast doubt as to a man's responsibility for the actions committed by a tulpa created by his thought and used as an instrument to further his designs. The double is an integral part of the individual, in other words it is "himself." He essentially created his double, therefore, responsibility for it rests in him.

Is this always truly so? Let's recall what has been said concerning doubles and especially tulpas who tend to free themselves of their dependence on their creator or on the individual to whom they are associated. Bear in mind their inclination to acquire a distinct personality, how they succeed in doing so, and the consequences that ensue. These are so many facts that the Tibetans hold as self-evident.

From this point the question of responsibility becomes more complicated. With whom does it lie when it is a question of a double that has become partially freed and has gone wandering far from the control of the individual to whom it is bound? What about the case of the tulpa that has become detached from its creator and whose actions no longer follow the impulses it receives? What about the tulpa that survives its creator? These questions give rise to animated controversies among the learned lamas, who are, by the way, not so very numerous.

A more specialized question of the order of those just listed is that concerning dreams. Tibetans believe that dreams are caused by the ramblings of the double that is set partially free by the passive state we enter when sleeping. Tsong Khapa, the reformer of the Tibetan clergy,[66] founder of the Gelegspa sect,[67] didn't hesitate in declaring that the acts committed in a dream entail the same consequences from the moral perspective as those committed in the waking state.

Others have seen this matter differently. The actions committed in dream, they say, neither entail culpability nor the awarding of merit. They denote our habitual inclinations, our desires, our thoughts at the time of dreaming and, in many ways, they reflect the contents of our most intimate *I*, the transitory composition of our being. Examining our dreams is educational and teaches us to know ourselves.

But what becomes of the acts that we commit in dreams, the feelings that we manifest there? Have they no result? You mustn't believe it.

Nothing of what appears or what manifests on one plane or another of existence can be erased or annihilated. Everything is in a state of continuous transformation, nothing endures and, at the same time, nothing is destroyed. The elements of the scenes that we see in dreams, the people we meet, the acts we commit are all parts of ourselves, linked to the multiple causes that have formed us and that tomorrow will constitute the new individual that we will be— not the same as the individual of yesterday and yet no different.

To be "responsible" means to be the "cause," to be a rebirth in an immortal series of rebirths.

---

66. Tsong Khapa was born around 1356 in Amdo, in northern Tibet.

67. Those who wear "virtuous dress," currently known as "yellow hats" because of the color of their hats.

INDIA

INDIA DOESN'T OFFER AS LUXURIANT A FIELD OF VARIOUS BELIEFS concerning the conditions of an individual's perpetual life as those we have so hastily explored in China and Tibet. This stems, without doubt, from the fact that the nature of the *ego*, whose duration is desired, is conceived by the majority of Indians, with the exception of the intellectual elite, in a similar fashion. Here, the most widespread belief concerning the ego or the individual is at first sight somewhat comparable to that expressed in the Catholic catechism: "Man is composed of a mortal body and an immortal soul."

However, the *jîva*, the vital principle that outlives the body, such as the Indians understand it, is fairly different from the soul and plays a different role. Whereas the soul, according to western belief, is created all of a piece at the birth of the individual, the jîva is very much the elder of the human body, the physical form that is introduced into the world at birth. In fact, it has been in existence for a period of time of inconceivable duration in which it has wended its way from one reincarnation to the next until the moment it appeared on the earth clad in human shape.[1]

---

1. It is born for the first time in a human form or else it has been previously reincarnated many times in this manner.

95

The nature of the human condition that befalls the individual is not an accident of chance. It is the result of a series of inflexible causes and their consequential effects. These causes are the physical and mental actions that have been accomplished in the past by the bodies (the individuals) that the jîva has successively inhabited.

The problem of a retributive system of justice finds itself thus managed in a very satisfactory manner. The fortunate circumstances that I enjoy are a result of my labor; I have built them around myself just as I've attracted all the misfortunes from which I suffer. Neither are effects visited upon me at the convenience or arbitrary will of a powerful being that is foreign to me.

The Indians cannot comprehend those foreigners who are incapable of providing a moral reason for the condition of a newborn who, according to their beliefs, has no personal past behind it. Why, these foreigners ask, are some born deformed and others beautiful, some intelligent and others obtuse? Who takes pleasure in creating and tossing individuals that are so different from one another out into the world?

The view of their individual duration in the past assures the Indians of their continued duration in the future. They will continue to wend their way through countless periods of time with stops of varying lengths in the different states of existence. Their thirst for perpetual life therefore appears to be satisfied. Is it truly? As we will see, it is nothing of the sort.

This quasieternity stretching out before them has frightened a minority of thinkers and, from the dawn of their religious history, Indians have envisioned a stop, an end, to this succession of reincarnations. It is liberation from this that the sages of India aim at. *Moksha* and *mukti*[2] are the names given to this "deliverance." This is

---

2. Nirvana.

the goal that those who are tired of "turning" on the wheel of repeated deaths and rebirths strive to attain.

However, those who truly feel weary of the succession of reiterated births that each of their deaths leads them to are not very numerous. They may complain of their fate but nourish the hope of a different destiny, the hope for happy days in their future life. The poor, despised pariah sees himself becoming a rich and honored Brahmin. Each individual, in his own way, tastes in advance the realization of his desires and, above all, is convinced that he will continue to live, that he will not *end*.

Clairvoyant masters have vainly denounced the painful conditions among which the lives of a great number of people unfurl,[3] the facts that throw this into relief are obvious—everybody is aware of them—but everyone accepts and submits to them rather than renounce living an individual life that stands out from its setting. They submit to them rather than renounce the tenacious illusion of being this *I*, this separate entity that one longs to continue being eternally.

The reincarnation of the jîva (the ego) is thus unanimously accepted by the average Hindu.[4] Few of them are capable of or even

---

3. "O disciples, what do you think is the mass of the waters of the great ocean or that of the tears you have shed during the course of your long pilgrimage, perpetually racing to new births and new deaths, joined to that which you hate and separated from that which you love? This wheel is without beginning and without end. Unknowable is the beginning of beings enveloped in ignorance, who impelled by desire are led toward rebirths, who pursue this wheel of rebirths. Thus, for a long time, you have suffered physical pains, moral sufferings, and fattened the soil of cemeteries. Long enough to have become disgusted with this existence, long enough to turn aside from it and free yourselves" (Samyutta Nikâya).

4. The qualification "Hindu" must be understood as applying to the Brahman religion and its worshipers. *Indian* signifies the nationality; the Muslims native to India, the Buddhists, the Parsis, and so on are Indians but not Hindus.

concern themselves with creating a perfectly clear idea of what this transmigrating jîva is.

According to popular belief, a person is reborn into the human species a very short time after his or her death. Rebirths in the world of gods or animals are not excluded, but they only figure in literature, legends, and tradition. We should not be astounded to find that the description given by the Indian to the situation of the disincarnate jîva has features similar to those we have already encountered in the previous chapter concerning the Bardo Thödal. As has been mentioned, the original text was Indian and translated by the Tibetans.

However, the popular Indian beliefs present hardly any trace of the philosophical tendencies expressed in the Bardo Thödal in regard to the journey that the namshés, the disincarnate jîva, accomplishes in the interval that separates the time of death from the moment of reincarnation.

Whereas the namshés of the recently deceased or dying Tibetan is urged to understand the irreality of the visions that appear and the purely subjective nature of the journey it seems to be undertaking, the Indian, apart from an intellectual elite, has no doubt whatsoever concerning the reality of the descriptions provided in their religious books that deal with the strolls of the disincarnate spirit and the incidents they include. A brief summary of these adventures will permit the reader to get a clear idea of the picture contemplated by an Indian when he thinks of the fate of the dead.

At the precise moment of death, a human has a sudden vision, as fleeting as a lightning flash, of absolute Unity, of the cessation of all distinctions, a vision of Existence in Itself in which *he is*, of which *he is* part, and that *he is*.[5] Following after instantaneously, the vital breath

---

5. This is the vision attained by the sages who wrote the Upanishads, which is expressed in the Advaita Vedanta. See the Bardo Thödal as well.

escapes the body, leaving it inanimate. Thus the journey begins.

Dragged by beings that appear as terrifying figures, the jîva is brought before Yama, the Lord of the Dead, who announces the future awaiting it as a result of the good and bad deeds that it has committed and also as a result of the thoughts and desires that occupied its mind at the time of death. However, the verdict that has just been rendered is not immediately carried out. Undoubtedly, the tale runs foul here of different versions of the voyage in the beyond. Here is one that is generally accepted.

The disincarnate jîva feels naked, it is famished. It hurls itself greedily on the rice cakes (*pinda*) that its relatives have prepared for it. This offering ritual, considered of the highest importance, is called *shrada*.

But the jîva doesn't merely have need of food. Deprived of the material body that clothed it, it must construct a new one in which to shelter itself until the moment arrives to be reincarnated. The shrada ritual therefore includes the symbolic offering of several threads torn from the clothing of one of the deceased's relatives and several of their hairs. "O father," the officiating priest says to the deceased, "may you be satisfied with this offering. Don't take any more from us."

This behest reveals the fear that the dead person inspires in the living, in his family. His fate is considered hardly enviable, and a regret for terrestrial life is attributed to him. He wishes, it is thought, to regain the condition that death has forced him to lose. He envies the living and wishes to appropriate their vital breath and live again.

However, though they were tenderly attached to the deceased, his relatives have no desire to surrender their own lives to him. He will be clothed and fed in the extraterrestrial regions where he has moved, but he must be content with what has been given him and not seek to take more.

Once the ceremony has ended, the ancestral Fathers are respectfully dismissed and the witnesses sweep the ground behind them while leaving to erase their tracks and thus prevent the deceased from following them back to his former dwelling and resuming his occupation. As long as he remains in the land of the dead, his presence is not desired . . . it is dreaded.

We have seen how the rural Tibetans manifest analogous feelings in an even more brutal fashion. But what is this land of the dead where the disincarnated sojourn? There is no unanimity of opinion on this subject or rather, it is imagined that not all of the dead inhabit the same place.

Particular offerings are anticipated for the Fathers who, respectively, live in different regions. The text recited during the shrada gives us information on this subject. This is it:

> Those of you, O Fathers, who are still in our world, those of you in the middle regions, and those of you who have earned the privilege of drinking amrita[6] may you all rise to the upper regions.
>
> Those of you, O Fathers, who have taken the form of vital breath, may you be purified. And may those Fathers who have attained knowledge of the Truth protect us.
>
> May the Fathers, the Grandfathers, and the Great-grandfathers who have eaten the food provided during the shrada, be satisfied.
>
> The Fathers are happy after having drunk and eaten. May they satisfy me by giving me the realization of my desires.
>
> May you be purified, O Fathers, by washing your hands.[7]

---

6. *Bhou* is our world; *Bhouva* is the atmosphere, the region of the ancestors *(Pitris)*; *Svarga* is paradise, the world of the gods who drink the beverage of immortality, amrita. This is equivalent to the Greek *ambrosia*. A contradiction can be pointed out here. In spite of the immortal nature of this drink, the gods, however prodigious their longevity, were mortal.

7. In accordance with Indian custom, where one washes one's hands after a meal, water is offered to the ancestors.

Fathers who live in this world and possess a body, Fathers who don't live
in this world. Fathers whom we know and Fathers whom we know
not, come participate in this sacred rite.
May the wind carry honey, may the rivers run with honey.[8]
May the plants produce honey.
May the nights be sweet as honey.
May the mornings be sweet as honey.
May the earth be sweet as honey.
May the heavens, the Father of us all, be sweet as honey.
Greetings to the spring, the summer, the rainy season, the autumn, and
the winter.
Greetings to you, O Fathers; give us large families.
We give you clothing, O Fathers. This clothing is a thread, please cover
yourselves with it.

I will add here some reflections of a Hindu scholar[9] concerning the
shrada:

It is certain that after the ritual is celebrated the ancestors are
beseeched to return to their respective homes and that the ground
of the site where the ritual took place is swept. But the base on
which this ritual is based is the immortality of the jîva and each
object offered in effigy during the course of the ceremony is
supposed to be used by the deceased in another world.[10]

It is imagined that for a certain interval of time (generally a year)

---

8. Throughout the following passages, honey signifies a pleasant sweetness.

9. Raj Bahadur Lala Baij Nath (now deceased).

10. From this belief comes the custom of sometimes offering jewels and even
truly personal objects to the deceased. Though the deceased supposedly receives
these gifts, they are in effect given to the Brahmins.

after death, the deceased lurks on the earth, depending on the offerings that are made to it for its food. These must be employed in the construction of a body suitable for residence in the world of the ancestors. After a year has passed, the deceased will convey itself to the world to which it has been assigned.[11]

I have quoted the opinion of my learned friend as appropriate for supporting the summary account that I have made of Hindu opinions and practices concerning the dead; but opinions and practices that relate to this subject are multiple and different though they all rest on the common belief of a semimaterial life of the dead in diverse regions of the beyond. What is this entity whose life it is a question of maintaining? Is it the jîva? As the Hindus believe that it is immortal, it hardly seems necessary to feed it. However, this jîva appears to have dragged a companion along with it while separating from the body. This companion is the ethereal body of the deceased.[12]

We could call this companion a double, such as that encountered in the preceding chapter. Some believe that this ethereal body, which doesn't die with the body, accompanies the jîva until the moment that the latter reincarnates in a new body in which it reincarnates as well. Others believe that the ethereal body only endures among those whose minds were still burdened with desire at the moment of death.[13]

---

11. Assigned in accordance with its appearance in Yama's court. See p. 108–109.

12. The *soushma sarira* that doesn't perish when the body dies.

13. The Tibetans urge the dying to declare those desires they still wish to satisfy, to disencumber their mind of all worries, and to entrust into the hands of their friends and family those actions they can no longer accomplish. It is important that they die with their spirits freed from all attachment and preoccupation. This is important for their future existence as well as for that of the living, whom the dead could annoy by virtue of their acts left either unachieved or only existing as projects yet to be undertaken at the time they quit the world.

The Indian belief in this subtle principle and the rituals based upon it date from a very great antiquity. The contemporary Hindu performing the shrada is doing nothing more than uttering liturgical phrases and performing ritual gestures that India has seen repeated identically for three thousand years.

In the time of the Vedas, not only the lower class Indians, but the intellectuals believed in the existence of a double associated with the body. The nature of this entity seems ill defined. Sometimes it was identified with the vital breath that manifests through respiration, sometimes with the principle of thinking, of knowing: the *manas*. Whatever the case may be, this principle, without being immortal, survived the death of the individual and following that event, had an independent existence. The entities left behind by our ancestors are the *Pitris* (the Fathers).[14]

Where are these Fathers to be found? What is their fate in the world in which they exist? They retain their own personality, but this personality is not uniform. One trait, however, is common to all: they possess a body and to maintain their existence, this body needs food. They even crave clothing. For want of being provided with the indispensable elements necessary for a continued life, the "Father," who appears to have a tenacious grasp on the conservation of that existence with an avidity that is equal to our own, can become a malevolent phantom.

However, Vedic antiquity knew a world other than that of the Pitris. This world welcomes a certain category of the dead. These are those who, in the course of their terrestrial life, have offered numerous ritual sacrifices and provided abundant gifts to the Brahmins. To these individuals the world of the gods is open.[15]

---

14. The *Manes* of the Greeks and Romans.

15. We will see (p. 112) that the father of Nachiketa offers a sacrifice consisting of all his possessions in order to be reborn among the gods. The idea of three

How is this world conceived? In a quite material manner. A hymn from the Ṛgveda lets us perceive the sojourn of delights toward which the aspirations of that faraway era were extended. It is a prayer addressed to Soma, the deity personifying the sacred beverage, soma.

> *The world where shines the inexhaustible splendor, where the sun is en-*
> *throned, enthrone me there, O Soma, in the imperishable world of*
> *immortality.*
> *Where lives the king, the son of Vivasvant, where lies the solid vault of*
> *the firmament, where the running waters are, in this place, make me*
> *immortal.*
> *Where one moves about at one's leisure, in the threefold firmament, in the*
> *threefold heaven of the heavens, where lie the worlds of light, make me*
> *immortal.*
> *Where desire and kindness exist, on the surface of the empurpled sky,*
> *where the banquet of the souls takes place and where there is an abun-*
> *dance of food, in this place, make me immortal.*
> *Where joy and delight reign, where reigns pleasure heaped upon plea-*
> *sure, where the heart's desires are attained, in this place, make me*
> *immortal.*

These guests of the gods and the gods themselves are nourished by the offerings made to them by the living. Their immortality therefore appears precarious. On the other hand, the pleasures taken by these guests of paradise are far from being only of a spiritual nature. They are promised numerous women and inexhaustible sexual prowess.

This quite material bliss is not the lot of all the deceased. The world of the Fathers, the *Pitri loka*, is sometimes represented in Vedic

---

worlds appears in the renunciation formula of the Indian sannyasins who renounce our world, the world of the ancestors, and the world of the gods: *bhou,*
bhouvar, and *sva.*

scriptures as a somber underground dwelling that is lit by neither the sun or the moon. This description is quite close to that of the Yellow Springs country that is encountered in China. The realm of Hades in Greek mythology was also a somber place.

Like the dead admitted to paradise, those who have descended into this darkened abode have been brought there in their semiphysical form, their double which must still be fed. A very detailed ritual indicates the manner in which the food—rice cakes and clear water—must be offered and the terms of the sacred formula with which they are presented. This denotes the extent of the belief that the donors think the Fathers possess to either procure them material advantage or injury. In exchange for the food that is offered, their descendants ask the Fathers to help them thrive, acquire wealth, a vigorous male posterity, and long life.

Not all the Fathers inhabit the paradises or the dark regions. A great number of them float in the atmosphere and invisibly surround those who remain on this earth. Here they wander around our dwellings or even lurk inside of them among the objects that they possessed in their lifetimes. They are also expressly singled out in the ancient as well as the modern ritual of the shrada. "Homage to you, O Fathers who dwell in space. / Homage to you, O Fathers who dwell on the earth," as the sacrificer has intoned for three thousand years while placing the offerings in the places and order prescribed.

These Fathers, possessing a body, have retained needs that are analogous to our own. Therefore in addition to food, they were offered medications, perfume, clothing, and even objects of furniture. These were never simulations as they are among the Chinese— paper money, paper horses, paper houses, etc. They are solid, real objects. The Fathers, it is supposed, make use of these objects' "doubles" that are made from a subtle matter that is analogous to that of their own double and suitable for it to utilize. What about the real and solid part of the objects: house, furniture, and so on? The Brahmin priests profited from these.

The custom of offering a piece of their clothing or several hairs from their bodies to the Fathers as raiment equally dates back to these long ago times.[16] The fear inspired by the semidisincarnated phantoms of the Pitris lurking around the living still continues. "Here is clothing for you, O Fathers, take nothing more from us for your use," Hindus would recite in the time of the Vedas. This same formula is repeated even today.

Those fathers not seated at the gods' banquet, and perhaps even those, still yearn for the lives they led among us and are ever on the watch for opportunities to take them back by assimilating the vital breath of the living. They are ready to become vampires. As such they are dreadful and feared by all. Their relatives fear they will only linger around them after having their wants satisfied. "You should be delighted, O Fathers. Now be on your profound ways."

Once the ritual has been completed, the participants shake the flaps of their clothing out of fear that a Father may have attached himself to their garments in order to continue lingering among the living. Then the place in which the ceremony took place is swept out. Thus, there are no traces left behind which the Fathers can refer which would give them the possibility of returning. The participants will remind them of the time ordained for the next feast, which will enable them to extend their precarious existence.

These individuals have not yet attained immortality in their present state. Contemporary and ancient Hindus alike share a vague

---

16. Commenting on this ritual, Max Muller observed that it was only practiced by the eldest, who were closer to the deceased than the other donors and who had a greater fear of being carried away by the Fathers.

idea of their fate, but they all express confidence in the declaration from the Bhagavad Gîta: "That which is cannot cease to be."

Let's study another, very popular, description of the jîva's journey. It is borrowed from the *Garuda Purana*. When on the brink of death, the human being has a sudden vision of Supreme Unity.[17] Next, the vital breath escapes and the envoys of the King of the Dead (Yama) extract the jîva from the body. The jîva is about the size of the thumb.

These envoys appear in terrifying shapes, armed with lassos and cudgels. Making terrible threats against the jîva, they carry it along the road to Yama's kingdom.

The jîva is starving and suffering from thirst, threatened by ferocious beasts, and beaten by its bearers. It is dragged unmercifully along a road that offers abrupt climbs and vertiginous descents at every turn. Then it can throw a rapid glance at Yama.

The jîva eats the cakes and drinks the water left as ritual offerings by its family. However, its hunger and thirst are not yet satisfied, but with their aid it will construct a new body fed by the funeral offerings that are made anew on the eleventh and twelfth days following the funeral.[18]

At this point, the jîva is again taken over long roads by the envoys of Yama who bring it before their king. During this long journey, the jîva again suffers from extremes of hot and cold and is threatened by wild beasts. It recalls the evil deeds it has committed while

---

17. Compare this description to that of the Bardo Thödal on p. 34.

18. Note that the numerous wanderings of the jîva occur in a very restricted allotment of time as do dream episodes, and like those, this voyage is very subjective. As to the sensations caused by this journey, it is believed that they are experienced by the ethereal body.

alive and is tormented by the painful consequences that they entailed for it. It looks in vain for a protector to come to its aid, but there is none to be found.

During the course of this journey, it subsists entirely on the monthly offerings of funeral cakes. At the end of six months it arrives at the edge of a river. A boat is moored at the banks, but before being allowed to take a seat in it, the jîva must furnish proofs of the good deeds it has accomplished. If it is unable to do so, it is thrown in the river, harpooned, and dragged like a fish the length of the river to Yama's city. This journey takes one year.

Yama's city has four doors; through them enter, respectively, those who have been charitable, wise, and brave. Sinners enter the city through the southern gate.[19]

The King of the Dead is seated on his throne surrounded by scholars, sages, and the good. Everything that surrounds him personifies Truth and Justice. Lies, injustice, and evil sentiments have no access to his city.

The king's minister, Chitragupta, has his own court and personal assistants who record all the deeds accomplished by each individual through word and action. A reading is done of the page concerning the individual appearing before this tribunal. Next, its sentence is pronounced. The person who has lived an evil life is condemned to suffer in the infernal worlds for a period of time that can be of an inconceivably long duration before reincarnating as a human being. This is sometimes only after having passed through several reincarnations as various animals.

---

19. In India as in Tibet, north is the sacred direction taken by the disincarnate souls to reach the dwellings of the gods or attain the supreme liberation "in which the man who knows the Brahman returns to the Brahman" (Bhagavad Gîta 10:24). In contrast, the south is considered unpleasant.

The jîva that finds itself again in a human womb will recall the circumstances of its previous lives. It will remember its desires, its mistakes, its evil deeds, and the harm that it has caused to others. It promises itself that it will not relapse into its old disastrous ways, which were the causes of the torments it had just endured.

It is born and gradually these memories grow more obscure. Then, still subject to the effect of the old tendencies encrypted within and of the ignorance it has been incapable of vanquishing, it begins to undiscernedly accumulate both good and bad actions that will carry it into the wheel (samsâra) of new deaths and births.

The "wheel" continues as well for those who, during their lives on earth, have been charitable, just, and so forth. These individuals leave Yama's court in sumptuous chariots that transport them to their celestial abodes. The description of their journey and that of the marvelous places where they live fill numerous pages of Indian literature. The various paradises are depicted with a wealth of material detail that denotes the attachment to physical pleasure of those who imagined them. There are immense gardens where the fortunate frolic with the gods. Hunger, thirst, and fatigue are never experienced there. Only pleasant sounds are to be heard there and only sweet smells are inhaled. Anger and old age are unknown. Unpleasant bodily functions are not manifested in these paradises. The garlands of flowers that adorn the guests of these happy regions never fade, and so on.

However, the length of time the jîvas sojourn in these lands of delights, even though in comparison to our scales can extend for countless centuries, is not infinite. The good effects of the acts that brought them to these paradises are exhausted, and their reincarnations follow suit, with all their constituent vicissitudes. Immortality has not been attained.

Yet those still greedy for the immortality of their little individual

I do not slacken in the pursuit of their quest. They will never slacken, undoubtedly.

What becomes of *I* when my body ceases to exist? What will become of this *I* that appears to me as a separate entity from my body, capable of recording the sensations it experiences and comparing them and figuring their causes? What finally becomes of this *I* in all its inexpressible significance?

We see that it is this concern that alarms Arthabhâya.[20] Here he questions Yajnavalkya:

"When the parts that make up the individual dissolve, when their activities cease functioning (when the individual dies), what becomes of their spirit," he asked.

"Take my hand, Arthabhâya," said Yajnavalkya. "Let's go somewhere secluded. Such a question should not be debated among the crowds."

Therefore, they drew away to continue their discussion.

We are not given any more than this to consider on this subject. The text continues: "They spoke of works." What they said has no relevance at all to Arthabhâya's question. "Through good deeds you become good and through evil deeds you become evil."

One commentator, Anandagiri, tells us that Yajnavalkya, in an oblique manner, let it be understood that the union with Brahman—the union of Being with the Absolute—could not be attained by means of one's achievements. What is strikingly clear in this account is that teachings concerning the fate of the jîva after death were strictly esoteric in nature and that initiates must abstain from divulging them in public.

The example of another questioner is given in the same Upanishad. This questioner is a woman. Here is the example:

---

20. Brihadaranyako Upanishad.

The illustrious sage Yajnavalkya—belonging more to legend than history—had resolved to retire into the forest and end his days there absorbed in meditation.[21] Yajnavalkya had two wives. He called upon his favorite of the two and confided his resolve to her.

"Maitreyi," said Yajnavalkya, "I wish to raise myself above my state as head of the household. I am therefore going to divide all my property between you and Katyâyana."

"O Venerable one," responded Maitreyi, "if the entire earth and all its treasures belonged to me, would that give me immortality?"

Yajnavalkya said, "Your life would become similar to that of the rich but this wealth would, in no way, procure you immortality."

Maitreyi replied, "Then in what way would this wealth serve me, if by its means I could not obtain that immortality you know?"

Yajnavalkya responded, "Listen, you have always been dear to me and what you have just said makes me cherish you even more. Come, sit down, I am going to explain this matter of immortality to you. Try to understand me."

A very long discourse follows. The doctrine revealed by Yajnavalkya to his immortality-seeking wife is the same one that will later be taught by the School of the Advaita Vedanta, which its adepts still teach today. This doctrine states that the Universe and each of our personal souls are Existence in Itself, the unparalleled Brahman. To

---

21. According to Indian religious code, the life of a Brahmin is composed of four stages. In childhood he receives the belt that marks his caste and begins his studies. When his studies are finished, he marries and fathers a family. In his old age he abandons his worldly goods and retires into solitude to devote himself to the practice of meditation. In addition, he is able to embrace the life of a *sannyasin* later and, having broken free of all attachments, wander about.

know and realize our fundamental unity with the Brahman is to have awareness of our immortality.

Following is the story of a more audacious inquisitor. What better informed authority than the King of the Dead for gaining information on the mysteries of the beyond? The sacred scriptures of India have preserved an account of the memorable conversation of Nachiketa with Yama. I quote:

A wealthy man and household head, Vajasravana, who desired to be reborn in the company of the gods, offered all his property in sacrifice. He had a son named Nachiketa. This latter, animated by an intense feeling of filial piety, said to himself, "He who would offer such a sacrifice should omit nothing. If he saves the least of things for himself, he will fall into the world ruled by suffering."

He asked his father: "Who are you going to give me to?"

Vajasravana didn't answer him. The young man repeated his question without obtaining a response. He repeated it a third time.

Then his father, in exasperation, cried out, "I will give you to Death!"

The father quickly repented of the promise he had made in a fit of anger.[22] But Nachiketa, who persevered in his feelings of filial piety, thought it unsuitable for his father not to honor his

22. This story gives us grounds to believe that at the time it was written down human sacrifices were performed in India. As to the date of the Katha Upanishad, from which this story is taken, it is very uncertain. This is not related to the sacrifices of widows who are burned alive in the same pyres that consume their husband's body, which have continued into modern times. The last ceremonial sacrifice appears to have taken place in Nepal, in honor of the Goddess Talejou, during the middle of the nineteenth century.

word. And so his father sent him to Yama's dwelling. (He sacrificed him.)

Now it happened that when Nachiketa[23] arrived before Yama's dwelling, the latter was absent and couldn't receive him with the ceremony that was prescribed by law. His ministers reproached him bitterly for this, and Yama offered his apologies to his honored guest.

"O Brahman, because you, as my venerable guest, have waited for three nights before my door without having received the simple hospitality you were due, homage will therefore be given to you.

Make three wishes. In payment for the three nights you have spent without receiving an honorable reception, these wishes will be granted."

"O Death," responded Nachiketa, "may Vajasravana's angry thoughts be soothed, may his mind become calm, may he feel not a whit of anger toward me, and welcome me as his son. This is the first wish I made."[24]

"By my grace," said Yama, "your father will think of you affectionately. Rest in peace tonight. Your father will welcome you with open arms when you are freed from the land of the dead."[25]

Nachiketa continued: "O Death, you know what celestial fire is.[26] Instruct me in this ritual. The inhabitants of paradise are immortal.[27] This is the second wish I have made."

---

23. His spirit, his jîva, or his ethereal body.

24. Nachiketa asks to be revived and returned among the living and back into his family.

25. When you are resuscitated.

26. This was a Brahmanic ritual through the accomplishment of which ascension to the realm of the gods could be obtained.

27. They enjoy, at least, a longevity so prolonged that on the human scale it is equivalent to immortality.

"I am going to teach you," said Yama. "Know, Nachiketa, that the fire that allows ascension to the divine worlds is located in the hollow of the heart."

And Yama explained to Nachiketa the material symbolism of the Brahmanic ritual called "The Celestial Fire." He added that, henceforth, this ritual would be known as "The Fire of Nachiketa."

"Here is your second wish, O Nachiketa. Now formulate the third."

The preceding is nothing but a preamble. Nachiketa now arrives at the subject that is closest to his heart.

"This is my question. Some say that a spiritual principle exists[28] that continues to exist after death. Others say that it doesn't exist. I desire to know which is correct. My third wish is to have you teach me about this."

"O Nachiketa," responded Yama, "since very ancient times the gods themselves have sought the answer to that question! This is an extremely subtle subject that is most difficult to comprehend. Ask of me something else, don't force me to answer you. Give me the freedom not to grant this wish."

"If the gods themselves have sought the answer to this question, if, as you say, O Yama, it is difficult to understand, no other master but you could be found to answer it and I have no other wish more important than this one."

"Ask for sons and grandsons that will live one hundred years, Nachiketa, ask for huge herds of livestock, elephants, or horses, ask for gold; ask the entire earth of me, ask me to let you live for

---

28. A jîva, a soul distinct from the constituent elements of the individual, separate from the body, the senses, the mental faculties, and the spirit; a kind of independent personality.

as long as you desire. If you know of even better things ask for them in addition to wealth and a long life. Be a king ruling over the immense earth. I will fill all your desires. All those desires it is very difficult to satisfy such as celestial nymphs with their chariots and musical instruments. They will serve you. I will give them to you, but don't force me to answer you concerning the state of the jîva after death."

"O Yama, all these pleasures will wear out. Man's life is brief and with it disappears the horses and all the rest, the dances and the songs. Wealth doesn't satisfy man, he will only enjoy it until the time you call upon him. Therefore, keep your chariots, your dances, and your music. The wish that I have expressed is the one that I choose."

"O Death, tell me the truth about that subject on which man entertains doubts. Tell me what there is to the great 'Beyond.'" Nachiketa desired only to know this secret.

Yama hadn't succeeded in overcoming his questioner's obstinacy. Bound by the promise that he had made, he had to respond to him. What would he say? His very long discourse, which is recounted in the Katha Upanishad in the marvelous and captivating style of these ancient scriptures, discusses the fundamental theory of Indian philosophy: the unity of the individual ego[29] with the Great Whole; the Existence in which exists all beings. All beings are manifestations of that inconceivable All that the Indians call Atman or Parabrahm. "They discuss," said Yama, "the subject of Atman. Some say he exists, the others say he does not and none see that they are Atman."

---

29. Or, rather, as we who believe ourselves individuals are dupes of an erroneous perception and sensations, it is a question of recognizing the identical natures of the *Jîvâtma* with the *Paramâtma;* the individual soul with the universal soul.

Would Nachiketa be satisfied with this response? No, without a doubt. No more than were the questioners preceding him and probably those who would follow him over the course of the centuries. But India has no other answer to give them.

We can now take a rapid glance at the methods whose objective is to obtain, if not immortality, at least a considerable prolongation of life. All philosophical schools, all religions have witnessed the birth of divergent branches around them, which by virtue of the adaptations and interpretations forced upon them by the prevailing tendencies of the areas in which they spread, have strongly travestied the initial theme of the mother doctrine. Yoga, perhaps, holds the record for "adaptations" of this sort. Under its name have been elaborated the most varied theories and practices, which are at times in complete contradiction to the declared aim of authentic Yoga.

In the spirit of its founder; Patanjâli, Yoga consists of the termination of the continual wanderings of the mind. "Yoga is the suppression of the fluctuations of the mind and the cessation of its modifications; *Citta vritti nirodha,*"[30] according to the opening formula of Patanjâli's fundamental work, which provides the definitive statement of his doctrine.

Yoga signifies "union." The union comprised by Yoga is exactly the same as that aimed at by the Vedanta, which has borrowed it from the ancient teachings of the Indian sages who have transmitted it to us through the Upanishads. We have reason to believe that this teaching is an expression of the concept that lies at the bottom of Indian thought; a primitive pantheism or panentheism.[31] It is not at

---

30. This declaration can be compared to that of Buddha extolling the cessation of mental "constructions" (samskaras) that the mind surrenders itself to.

31. Two contemporary Indian philosophers, Satischandra Chatterjee and

all a question of individual immortality but of eternity in the in-conceivable infinity of the Atman-Existence in which we are and *that we are.*

We have seen that this perspective in no way satisfies the minds of those who are desirous of assurance in regard to the eternal continuation of their actual *I.* The reincarnation promised them by the system whereby the jîva "changes its dwellings" appears equally unsatisfactory to them because of the intervals of time existing between successive lives and the uncertainty of the mystery that hovers over the fate of their *I* during these intervals. Finally, it fails to satisfy them because of the memory loss that prevents the jîva from the possibility of relinking the events in which they have been involved in previous lives to their *I* of today. They can look forward to this same impossibility to be repeated with all their future reincarnations.

One division of Yoga, Hatha Yoga, appears to provide for the use of candidates for immortality several suitable means for the attainment of that goal. In truth, the treatises of Hatha Yoga hardly stress these practices, and they can remain almost invisible among the abundance of practices extolled for purifying the vital centers of the organism and producing mental stability by the mastery of respiration.

In the commentary annexed to the text of Swami Swatmaram's work, the *Hatha Yoga Pradipika,* a work that is viewed as an authority, it can be read:

Dhirendramohan Datta, in their commentary on Hymns 10 and 90 of the Ṛgveda write on this subject: "God imbues the world, but he is not entirely contained within it. He remains outside of it. In the terms of Western theology this concept is panentheism and not pantheism. The 'All' is not the totality of God but is contained within he who is larger than this 'All'" (*An Introduction to Indian Philosophy,* University of Calcutta, 1944).

Hatha is considered a name composed of two syllables. *Ha* signifies the moon and *tha* signifies the sun.[32] These correspond to the breath that flows through the right and left nasal passageways. The control of breathing with the aim of restricting fluctuation in the thinking principle is called Hatha Yoga.

It would not be wise to consider Hatha Yoga simply a dangerous form of gymnastics because it has been found that a moderate practice of its exercises is effective in the production of good health and longevity. Hatha Yoga brings with it the power of preventing both physical and mental illnesses. Its regular practice acts on the heart, the lungs, and the circulatory system. It even bestows the power of delaying death for an indefinite period of time. However, this ability is realer employed by the true Yogi who understands the consequences of opposing natural law.

Hatha Yoga places a great emphasis on the exercises of breath mastery in its system of physical and spiritual training. As a reference that testifies to the efficacy of the practices they teach, the masters of Hatha Yoga cite this text: "Brahma and the gods have devoted themselves to the practice of pranayama and are thus freed from fear of death; we should also adopt this practice."

Pranayama[33] is the name that has been given to the respiratory exercise applying to inhalation, exhalation, and, especially, the retention of the breath for as long a time as possible. A very large number of Indians, no matter the religious sect they belong to, practice this exercise on a daily basis. The effects they expect are extremely varied but often of a physical nature. Some believe, however,

---

32. Here can be found the idea of Yin and Yang from Chinese philosophy.

33. Pranayama includes *powata* (inhalation), *rechaka* (exhalation), and *kumbaka* (the retention of air that has been inhaled).

that breath retention produces mental and spiritual results that lead to mental concentration, ecstatic *samâdhis* (mystical raptures), and bestows magical powers.

Yogis have also found in this practice a means of suicide that occurs in the course of a state of intense bliss brought about by suffocation which, according to them, forces the vital breath to engage, throughout the entire body, the mystical arteries that cause it to rise to the upper center. This "lotus of one-hundred-thousand petals," located at the crown of the head, figures in all the systems of Indian physical culture.

However, before attaining this upper center, the breath must have been sent out throughout the body by the path of the three mystical arteries and touched upon the various vital centers. Here we find a theory and practice that is analogous to that of the Taoists, but in Hatha Yoga it is not a question of feeding the body through the absorption and "eating" of air, that is, assimilating it while it traverses the body. Hatha Yoga envisions this air circulation as a cleaning process that rids the *nadis*[34] of the impurities that prevent the free circulation of vital energy. This purification acts on the mind and prepares it for the attainment of spiritual illumination.

However great an importance is given in Hatha Yoga to respiration exercises, it is but one of the numerous exercises invented by the experts of that school. The majority of these exercises have no connection to our present subject—immortality—and we will not concern ourselves with them. I will restrict myself to mentioning those that give evidence of the obstinate nature of the quest for personal immortality, even by the most bizarre means.

An example is the elongation of the tongue; the flesh securing

---

34. Particularly in the three principal arteries of the mystical anatomy along which is said to circulate the vital energy, respectively known as *ouma, roma,* and *kyangma.*

the tongue is gradually cut away, a little each day, until the tongue is entirely free and can twist itself in such a manner that it can reach the extreme edge of the palate and cork the opening of the canal that serves to conduct air into the lungs. The tongue when stretched out should be able to touch the point located between the eyebrows and also to touch the ears.

It is said that six months of these daily exercises are the minimum necessary toward achieving satisfactory results. The yogi who has perfected it and is capable of remaining, even for only a half a minute, with his tongue twisted around while holding his breath is, we are assured, freed from illness, old age, and even death. Another result of this exercise is depicted in the following extract: "Once the yogi has sealed the opening of the windpipe, his semen will not escape, even when he is tightly clasped in the arms of a young and passionate woman."

Let's note that the retention of seminal fluid, like that for breath, figures among the means that are judged suitable for increasing longevity, if not even capable of leading to immortality. The masters who teach Hatha Yoga believe that it is through the loss of semen, as with breath, that man's vital substance escapes. The candidate for immortality is therefore compelled to conserve both of these within in order to feed from them. To this effect a complicated system of various practices concerning sexual union has been elaborated. Among these is the practice that aims to increase the sum of energy contained in the semen and to cause it to rise along the nadis until it reaches the vital center located at the crown of the head, just as it is claimed air can be made to rise through breath retention in the practice of pranayama.

Hatha Yoga doesn't fail to turn its attention to *Kundalini*, the energy *(shakti)* that sleeps, like a coiled serpent, in the lower vital center located beneath the belly. Numerous methods are indicated for awakening this energy, "to make the serpent uncoil," and force it to raise itself through the mystical veins to the ever sought objective of the superior center located at the crown of the head.

It is recommended that the bizarre techniques presented in the treatises of Hatha Yoga are not taken too much at face value. A great many of them are presented in symbolic and figurative terms that are only intelligible to the initiate. According to these adepts, a number of the methods that appear to the profane as applicable to the body in reality concern a mental or spiritual activity and the objects mentioned are completely different from those that bear the same names in ordinary language.

The fact cannot be denied however, that Hatha Yoga prescribes numerous exercises that are truly physical and that an equally large number of adepts in India devote themselves to their practice. Among these singular practices can be cited the practice of making the intestines move in a circular fashion within the lower abdomen, bringing them in a mass above the navel;[35] the elevation of the body with the legs straight in the air by resting on the head and supporting the haunches with the hands. Practicing this exercise on a daily basis while gradually increasing its duration will lead, after a somewhat long period of time, to the conquering of death. Other exercises when practiced assiduously over the years should lead, if not to immortality, at least to a continued existence that can be extended at will indefinitely.

The masters of Hatha Yoga warn those tempted to use these practices to delay the moment of death or gain immortality that this is regarded as extremely dangerous for their "spiritual health" because it denies the law of karma. By way of a conclusion, I will say

---

35. The efficacy of this practice in facilitating digestion and preventing constipation appears to have been proven.

that even though yogis are mentioned who, at an unspecified period, generally very long ago, have attained longevity of an unbelievable duration, none are cited who are reputed to be currently living immortals in the fashion of the Chinese Immortals.

As a useful supplement to what has just been said concerning Yoga and its respiratory practices, I include two quotations for which I am indebted to some contemporary Indian scholars.[36]

> Several spiritual masters, continuing efforts that have been pursued for thousands of years, have established five ways for attaining the primordial light. These are the five schools of philosophy and mental training that are known as: Sankya, Yoga, Pasupatam, Pancharatram and Smritimatam. The creators of these five schools have all recognized the importance of Yoga.
>
> Kumbaka, total breath retention, is achieved through mastery of respiration (pranayama), and through kumbaka laya is achieved a state of consciousness in which one is plunged into the Supreme Principle at the expense of his or her own identity.
>
> It is almost impossible to determine the era in which the various authors of the Yoga schools fundamental works lived, but it can be verified through personal experience the power to attain laya is a fact.[37]

Since time immemorial, the progressive mastery of respiration has been practiced as a means of achieving various objectives of religious discipline, including the highest of these goals: the breaking of psychophysical bonds. Breath mastery gradually leads to the

---

36. Through the friendly efforts of Madame Mira Alfeassa, founder of the Sri Aurobindo ashram in Pondicherry.

37. Translated from Tamil by Shri pandit, Nilakantha Mahadeva Joshi.

state of *samâdhi* (total mental concentration), which is its ultimate result. Among the Taoists it includes a cosmic sense concerning the production and transformation of cosmic value, which is to say, emancipation from cosmic energy loss and access to the highest degrees of psychic power which in turn leads to immortality.

Breath (in this meaning of the term) ought not be strictly assimilated into the physiological functioning of respiration. Breath is the supreme reality, the intrinsic movement, and the creative power. Through the exercising of this little mortal breath and elevating it to the necessary level, one can transform that which is imperfect, coarse, and imperfect in oneself into something that is pure and immortal.

All of these exercises require one to advance prudently and under the direction of a competent guide. These practices use two potent cosmic forces: *vâyu* and *agni*, wind and fire respectively. Putting them into play can produce results that are much worse than simple failure if the necessary balance between them is not maintained. Agni illuminates and also devours. Vâyu moves and carries off, but to where and for what reason? Where is the soma[38] that nourishes, satisfies, and provides realization? Modern nuclear science and its applications are currently heading for a collision with a similar question.[39]

---

38. The beverage offered to the gods during a sacrifice and also that which they drink in their celestial dwelling places.

39. Summarized in accordance with a note by Swami Pratyagatmanada, an authority on Tantric Yoga.

CONCLUSION

I DON'T FEEL QUALIFIED TO PASS JUDGMENT ON ANY OF THE DIFFER-
ent ways of imagining immortality and the means suitable to
achieving it, which we have encountered in the rapid and general
survey just completed. I will confine myself to citing opinions that
have been expressed to me by two men of completely different races
and cultures, living in equally different surroundings. One of these
individuals, a Tibetan contemplative hermit (gomchen), spoke to
me in a cave in a mountainous vale, which had been summarily contrived to serve him as a dwelling. The other was an Indian scholar
and a graduate of an American university.

The gomchen told me:

> Those wishing to convince themselves of their own immor-
> tality by basing it on reincarnations and the memories they
> have—or claim to have—of their past lives are off course. They
> believe that their *I* is a homogenous block, whereas it is, as taught
> in Buddhism, an aggregation[1] whose constituent elements are

---

1. The five physical and mental aggregations are the body, sensations, perceptions,
mental constructions (ideas and volition), and consciousness or knowledge.

essentially transitory in nature and have only a momentary exist-ence that is dependent on multiple causes.[2]

It is absurd to say that *I am* a reincarnation of Tsong Khapa, Srong bstan Gampo,[3] or any other person. However, the groups that have lived under the name Tsong Khapa, Srong bstan Gampo, or any other individual were made up as we are of sensations, perceptions, and consciousnesses.[4]

The activity of these elements, like all other physical and mental activities, engenders forces (energies).[5] These radiate outward and enounter propitious conditions and receptive groups (individu-als) that they incorporate themselves into. Thus, they reincar-nate and continue their existence.

Therefore, you shouldn't say, "*I have been* Tsong Khapa" or "*I have been* Srong bstan Gampo," but you are permitted to think that such a perception, such a sensation, or such a leap of aware-ness that you are currently experiencing could have been experi-enced by either one of these individuals among others. Currently,

---

2. Causes that are both near and far in time and space; causes whose effects are manifested shortly afterward and those whose effects occur after a long delay; direct and indirect causes.

3. Tsong Khapa, the reformer of the Tibetan clergy, was born in 1356. Srong bstan Gampo, an illustrious king of Tibet, was born around 617.

4. Consciousness in Buddhism signifies the ability to become aware of a mental or physical object inscribed in the spirit; that's to say, a grasp of awareness incor-porated into the substance of the ego. The transitory elements of our group are capable of transmitting to their successors the impressions they have felt or their effects, as well as the physical and mental modifications of which they can be comprised. There are mental memories that are sometimes conscious and some-times unconscious. There are physical memories of which we remain unaware unless we exert ourselves to bring them up to the level of clairvoyant conscious-ness. Heredity and atavism are forms of memory.

5. *Shug* (*shugs*) or *tsa* (*rtsal*).

they are manifesting the persistence of their own existence through the intermediary of the group that I call *I*.

Moreover, we don't inherit our predecessors exclusively as guests within us. Perceptions, sensations, consciousness—awarenesses travel throughout the world and are not truly the property of anyone of us.

I brought up the question of "déjà vu," the impression felt by some people that they have already found themselves in a place or circumstances that they have had no previous contact with. I was referring to the impression often proffered in the West that the person who had the impression of having already been in such and such a spot or in analogous circumstances recalls, in reality, tales that they have heard or images they have seen, whose memory had been submerged into their subconscious.

This could be so, my interlocutor responded, but the "awareness" of having been in this place or those circumstances *has existed*, it has been experienced by certain individuals, it has been able to transmigrate and "reincarnate" in the person currently experiencing it and manifest itself in the form of more or less lucid memories.

All that has been remains.

The Indian intellectual, ably equipped from his American education, has given me quite extensive explanations, which I summarize as follows:

It is difficult to discern the boundary—limit that exists between "living" and allegedly inanimate matter. As far as the origin is concerned of the first living thing that has differentiated and disengaged itself from nonliving matter, it remains as unknown today as it was in the era when Buddha declared, "The origin of beings is without known beginning."

However, what we can be certain of is that the various actions and reactions that have constituted the activity of beings for as long as the millions of years that their evolution has lasted, have left, in one form or another, traces in the constituent substance of each presently existing being. Active forces transmitted by our ancestors and living in us have been reincarnated there.

Undoubtedly, we cannot trace the long line of these reincarnations back indefinitely, even though we can find a solid support for our convictions from scientific assumptions. However, through meditation and through assiduous and lucid introspection, we can manage to discern thoughts, ways of seeing, the presence of multiple personalities that are active in us in the form of impulses who are the constituent elements of our present *I*. Through its intermediary, we are assured an incommensurable and perhaps eternal existence by living on in our successors in our turn.

What is cannot cease to be.

INDEX